International Trade Centre

Product and market development

Silk Review 2001

A survey of international trends in production and trade

Sixth edition

Geneva 2002

ABSTRACT FOR TRADE INFORMATION SERVICES

2002 SITC 261
SIL

INTERNATIONAL TRADE CENTRE UNCTAD/WTO (ITC)
Silk Review 2001: A survey of international trends in production and trade. Sixth edition
Geneva: ITC 2002. xi, 47 p.

Survey of world production and trade of silk, silk yarn, silk fabrics and silk clothing – provides overview of production, international trade, consumption, generic promotion of raw silk and various silk products; examines effect of ecological factors of silk trade; reviews consumer markets in selected EU countries, Switzerland, Japan, USA and United Arab Emirates; gives overview of production and trade in selected silk-producing countries and areas focusing on the role of China in international silk trade – reviews market situation and characteristics; other silk-producing countries and areas covered include Africa, Brazil, India, Republic of Korea, Thailand, Viet Nam, Bangladesh, Colombia, Nepal, Uzbekistan, Japan, United Kingdom. Tables provide statistical data and prices.

Subject descriptors: **Silk, Statistical data, World, European Union, France, Germany, Italy, Switzerland, United Kingdom, Japan, United States, United Arab Emirates, China, Brazil, India, Korea R, Thailand, Viet Nam, Africa, Bangladesh, Colombia, Nepal, Uzbekistan.**

English, French (separate editions)

ITC, Palais des Nations, 1211 Geneva 10, Switzerland

Digital image on the cover: © International Silk Association. The image shows children's costumes for the Celebration of Costumes Festival in Japan.

ITC/P144.E/PMD/MDS/02-IX

ISBN 92-9137-244-7
United Nations Sales No. E.02.III.T.8

Foreword

This is the sixth edition of the survey of trends in international silk production and trade, which the International Trade Centre UNCTAD/WTO (ITC) has been publishing since September 1988. It updates the statistical data presented in the 1997 edition and reviews the roles of developing and other countries in the international silk trade as these have evolved since then.

This comprehensive study was prepared by Antero Hyvärinen, an ITC staff member who retired from service in 2001. His technical contribution to the organization's work in the promotion of trade in silk and silk products for over 15 years has been highly valued, as has his close cooperation with many organizations such as ISA, ISC, UNIDO, FAO, ESCAP, the World Bank and several national associations in both developing and developed countries.

The last 15 years have been an era of great changes in the international silk trade. When ITC started its activities in this sector a relatively small selection of finished silk goods could be found in exclusive retail shops. These items were mostly produced by top European silk-processing companies in France, Italy, Switzerland and the United Kingdom. At the time, China was by far the largest producer of raw silk, as it is still today – but the country is no longer primarily an exporter of raw silk and semi-finished products, such as silk yarn and loomstate silk fabrics (grège). In 1985 some 40% of China's silk exports were raw silk and silk yarn, and 37% silk fabrics. The share of finished silk goods, such as garments and accessories, was 23%. In 2000 the corresponding figures were 33% for raw silk and silk yarn, 17% for silk fabrics and 49% for finished goods. Thus, China has developed its silk industry towards silk processing instead of remaining as a raw material source for the rest of the world.

In the early 1990s the silk world experienced a new phenomenon: a special treatment of silk, which made it soft and without the traditional shine – sand-washed silk. A large variety of silk garments, for both men and women, were introduced at affordable prices for sale in department stores, mail-order houses and even in some coffee shops. This trend changed the image of silk, particularly in Europe. Silk was for the first time affordable for large consumer groups. No doubt the low prices and poor quality of sand-washed silk garments (especially towards the end of the boom) had a negative effect on the image of both and subsequently the international silk trade. It remains to be seen how the silk trade will evolve in the coming years, but it is necessary to try to ensure that consumers will be offered new, interesting and qualitatively attractive products. As silk is and will remain a very scarce commodity, amounting to less than 0.2% of all textile fibres, everything should be done to guarantee a good use of this fibre. One should also keep in mind the labour-intensive nature of sericulture and silk production. As poverty eradication is one of the important activities for the United Nations, efforts should continue to support raw silk production in developing countries and transition economies.

Since the mid 1980s, some well-known traditional silk producers, notably Japan and the Republic of Korea, have stopped commercial production of raw silk. The ongoing industrialization in these two countries made it impossible to continue to produce raw silk locally, but some silk processing still remains, especially in the Republic of Korea.

Under forthcoming liberalization of the international trade in textiles and clothing at the end of the WTO Agreement on Textiles and Clothing (ATC) on 31 December 2004, all the existing quota restrictions to this trade will be removed by that date. This will not directly change international silk trade: China is the only silk producer placed under quota restrictions by the European Union and the United States. However, an indirect impact will be the competition from other textiles that are presently under quota restrictions. Existing tariff barriers will have to be lowered in various developing countries. In India, for example, the huge market for sari fabrics, which has so far been well protected, may face new competition.

There are certain areas, such as silk promotion, where silk producers and processors could be more active. Over the years there has been much discussion about promotion, but funds have not been made available. Environmental matters are becoming increasingly important in international trade in textiles and clothing, and silk could possibly benefit from this trend. It is hoped that eventually something will be done in this respect, at least at a national level.

Acknowledgements

This survey was prepared by Antero Hyvärinen, ITC Senior Market Development Officer, who retired at the end of 2001. Matthias Knappe, who succeeded Mr Hyvärinen as Senior Market Development Officer, finalized the survey. Mr Knappe is responsible for ITC's trade promotion and development activities on clothing and textiles.

Alison Southby copyedited the book. Carmelita Endaya prepared the copy for printing.

Contents

Tables

Note

Unless otherwise specified, all references to dollars ($) are to United States dollars. All references to tons are to metric tons.

The following abbreviations are used:

ATC	Agreement on Textiles and Clothing
ESCAP	United Nations Economic and Social Commission for Asia and the Pacific
EU	European Union
FAO	Food and Agriculture Organization of the United Nations
ISA	International Silk Association
ISC	International Sericultural Commission
ITC	International Trade Centre UNCTAD/WTO
SITC	Standard International Trade Classification
UNCTAD	United Nations Conference on Trade and Development
UNIDO	United Nations Industrial Development Organization
WTO	World Trade Organization

Introduction

Brief history of silk

The history of silk can be traced back to China in the third millennium before the Christian era, where there is evidence of a written symbol for silk as early as 2600 BC. Fragments of Chinese silk fabrics have been found that date back to around 1500 BC. The oldest known writings on silk are of a more recent period and are found in the Indian epic the Ramayana, which was composed in 300 BC.

Silk was introduced to the West only during the reign of the Chinese emperor Wu-ti in 140–86 BC, when the beginnings of the famed 6,400-kilometre Silk Road were established. Towards the beginning of the Christian era raw silk began to be exported from the east to Rome, where it was literally worth its weight in gold.

Sericulture began in Byzantium in about the sixth century AD and, especially after the Crusades, spread to Italy (Sicily), Spain and France. By the fourteenth century, the Italian cities of Genoa, Florence and Lucca had become fabled weavers of silk fabrics. These were used only by the very affluent, who encouraged silk-weaving in the country. In France, in the latter half of the fifteenth century, Louis XI took positive measures to support the domestic industry, one of which was to limit imports from Italy. Lyon became a major centre for silk weaving, and by the end of the eighteenth century this city had 1,800 silk looms. The French Revolution brought about a complete cessation of production, and the silk industry in France was not to revive until the reign of Napoleon.

In the 1930s, the United States was by far the world's leading consumer of silk and Japan the largest supplier of the raw material. Demand came almost exclusively from producers of silk stockings until the outbreak of the Second World War and the cessation of silk deliveries from Japan. All the silk then available was used in the production of parachutes and products other than hosiery.

By the end of the 1920s sericulture in Japan was the mainstay of the foreign trade and in 1930 some 40% of the country's households were raising silkworms, producing 399,000 tons of silkworm cocoons. Following the emergence of synthetic fibres, however, demand for silk began gradually to drop.

Half a century ago, Japan's annual cocoon output was still more than 280,000 tons, from which 43,150 tons of raw silk were produced. This was well over half of the world's raw silk production. By 2000, Japan's output of raw silk was down to about 560 tons; long traditions in silk production in Japan have almost come to an end.

The invention and commercial introduction of nylon in 1938 shifted demand away from silk as a raw material for hosiery. By the end of the Second World War nearly all the stockings sold on the market were fashioned from nylon.

Silk and silk products have always been associated with luxury and have traditionally been expensive. The rearing of silkworms continues to be extremely labour-intensive and time-consuming. This, combined with the land requirements for mulberry plantations, makes silk production uneconomic for countries with high labour costs or little available land. However, the perception of sericulture as a profitable venture is encouraging countries with available labour, suitable climates and sufficient land to start sericultural activities.

The question of new countries venturing into sericulture and silk production has been discussed at various international forums, such as the XXVIIIth International Sericultural Congress of the International Sericultural Commission in Cairo, Egypt, in October 1999. The overwhelming consensus at the congress was that, as sericulture was not a simple agricultural activity, countries should not aspire to become silk producers unless they meet the following preconditions:

- They already have some tradition of carrying out this highly disciplined activity.
- They have silk-processing facilities, as the international market for silk cocoons seems to be disappearing.
- There should be a reasonably steady local demand for silk products.

There are ongoing projects either to revive national traditions of sericulture and silk production (a World Bank funded sericulture/silk production and marketing project in Bangladesh) or to start these activities in countries that are newcomers to the business (Bolivia and Peru). In Central Asia, countries such as Uzbekistan and Kyrgyzstan are gradually trying to revive their sericulture and silk-processing industries following the disappearance of their long-standing business contacts in the former Soviet Union.

Aims and scope of the survey

The purpose of this survey is to present an overall view of world production and trade and to make some projections concerning products and markets.

Unlike cotton and wool, which are typical export commodities and which are often processed in third countries, silk has traditionally been processed and consumed in the producing countries. Silk used to be mainly a raw material for luxury products. Today, however, silk goods have attracted a new consumer group – a young generation of consumers with more money to spend, partly because the number of women employed has increased dramatically during the last two decades. Another reason for the interest in silk is the general rise in demand for natural fibres brought about by the ongoing environmental movement.

The international silk trade has itself undergone a fundamental change in the last decade and a half. The introduction of sand-washed silk in the early 1980s 'democratized' the trade and brought silk within the reach of most consumers in the West. However, the low-cost goods did not live up to the traditional image of silk as a quality product. In the aftermath of that fashion wave, silk now has to compete with other textiles for a place in the international market.

Nevertheless, growing demand for ready-made articles in silk continues to encourage manufacturers in developing countries to try to penetrate markets in the West. Entry is normally achieved in close cooperation with the buyers – in Europe, the United States, Japan and other countries – who give producers detailed manufacturing instructions. In an attempt to give an overview of this development, this survey focuses on the following aspects:

- Major silk-producing countries;
- Major silk-consuming countries;
- Major exporters of silk products;
- Some projections on the future of the international silk market.

Survey methodology

This survey updates *Silk Review 1997*. It puts together available statistical data and information gathered from numerous interviews with silk producers, processors and traders in various parts of the world in 2000–2001. The interviews have been invaluable in giving a more reliable overview of general trends in the international silk trade. Among the information sources for the survey are the following:

- International Silk Association (ISA);
- International Sericultural Commission (ISC);
- National offices for the export promotion of silk and silk products in developing and other silk-producing countries;
- Individual silk exporters in developing and other countries;
- Silk importers, traders and converters in developed countries;
- United Nations agencies dealing with sericulture and silk production, such as the Food and Agriculture Organization of the United Nations (FAO), the United Nations Industrial Development Organization (UNIDO), the United Nations Economic and Social Commission for Asia and the Pacific (ESCAP) and the World Bank;
- Import promotion offices in Europe.

The ISA Secretariat, with which ITC has regular contacts, has been particularly helpful in the preparation of the survey.

Product description

In this survey the term 'silk' is used for mulberry silk, that is, silk produced by the mulberry silkworm *Bombyx mori*, unless a special reference is made to wild silks, i.e. *tussah, tasar, muga* and *eri*. The following categories of products are dealt with:

SITC Rev. 3 heading*	*Product description*
261.3	*Raw silk (not thrown)*
651.92	*Silk yarn (other than yarn spun from silk waste) not put up for retail sale*
654.1	*Fabrics, woven, of silk or of silk waste*
841–846	*Articles of apparel and clothing accessories for women, men and children*

* Standard International Trade Classification.

The term 'silk products' covers raw silk and further processed silk goods up to and including fabrics. The term 'made-up silk goods' refers to finished articles made of silk. The survey emphasizes dyed and printed silk fabrics for garments, ready-made garments, fabrics for interior decoration, and other products such as neckties, scarves, cushion covers and other items for the home.

CHAPTER 1

Overview of major findings

Production

Raw silk

Silk production is insignificant in comparison with that of other textile fibres, as table 1 clearly indicates. The share of silk in world production of all textile fibres in 1999 remained unchanged from its 1995 level of about 0.2%. Silk will never be available in large quantities and international supplies will no doubt remain limited in the future. This view continues to be supported by the information from China, where the growing domestic demand for silk products will eventually affect supplies available for export. In addition, a significant relocation of mulberry growing and silkworm breeding is under way in the country as industrialization continues apace.

Table 1 World production of textile fibres, by quantity, 1975–2000 (in thousands of tons)

Year	Cotton	Synthetics	Cellulosic fibres	Wool	Silk	Total
1975	11 809	7 346	2 959	1 502	49	23 665
1980	13 981	10 476	3 242	1 608	55	29 372
1985	17 540	12 515	2 999	1 673	59	34 786
1991	20 830	16 440	2 860	1 940	75	42 145
1995	19 200	20 200	3 000	1 600	100	44 100
1999	19 200	28 300	2 700	1 400	76	51 400

Source: UNSD/ITC Comtrade Database System, 2000.

Production figures for the world's leading producers of raw silk in various years between 1938 and 1999 are given in table 2. While world production rose by more than 100% between 1978 and 1993, it dropped by 30% from 100,000 tons in 1993 to 70,000 tons in 2000. The positions of China and India as first and second largest producers remain unchanged. Production in Japan continues to fall and in 1999 was about 2.5% of its 1938 level.

More than 70% of China's output is bivoltine silk, which is necessary for producing much of the silk required for international trade. In India, more than 95% of the silk produced is multivoltine (tropical). China had an output of about 50,680 tons of raw silk in 2000, a drop of more than 10% from 55,990 tons in 1999.

Table 2 World production of raw silk (mulberry), by country/area and by quantity, 1938–2000 (in tons)

Producer	1938	1978	1986	1992	1995	1997	1999	2000
Total of which:	**54 675**	**45 125**	**62 460**	**82 419**	**105 138**	**79 590**	**76 290**	**71 163**
China	4 855	19 000	35 700	54 480	77 900	55 117	55 990	50 683
India	690	3 475	8 280	12 600	12 884	14 048	13 944	15 214
Brazil	35	1 250	1 680	2 280	2 468	2 120	1 554	1 389
Uzbekistan	1 900	3 240	4 020*	2 160	1 320	2 000*	923	1 100
Thailand	n.a.	n.a.	n.a.	1 589	1 313	1 039	1 000	955
Japan	43 150	15 960	8 220	5 100	3 240	1 920	649	557
Republic of Korea	n.a.	n.a.	1,680	910	346	146	28	15
Viet Nam	n.a.	n.a.	n.a.	n.a.	2 100	834	780	n.a.
Democratic People's Republic of Korea	n.a.	n.a.	n.a.	1,200	600*	200	150	n.a.
Iran, Islamic Republic of	n.a.	n.a.	n.a.	423	750	500	n.a.	n.a.
Other	4 045	2 200	2 880	1 677	2 217	1 666	1 272	1 250

Source: ISA.

* Estimate.

As in Japan, silk production in the Republic of Korea continues to decline, largely because of industrialization. Labour-intensive sericulture has become too costly in these two countries and they now have to rely increasingly on imported silk to meet domestic needs. Japan remains one of the world's largest markets for silk products and its imports of silk products continue to rise. The Republic of Korea maintains an ample silk-processing capacity; it is now importing silk yarn and grey fabrics to be finished for export. The quality of printing silk fabrics in particular has improved in the country and finished silk fabrics, ladies' silk scarves and men's silk neckties have been exported in increasing quantities.

The 2000 output of Brazil (some 1,389 tons of raw silk), a comparative newcomer to the silk trade, was about 40% or almost 1,000 tons less than the 2,360 tons attained in 1996. The country's role as a supply source for Japanese silk processors has suffered a setback because of the declining demand for raw silk and silk yarn in Japan. The growing imports of finished silk products into Japan are gradually replacing local silk processing, i.e. silk weaving, dyeing and printing of silk and the production of silk garments and accessories.

Fabrics

Silk fabrics are produced either on hand-looms or on power looms. The bulk of the silk woven in China comes from power looms; production in Thailand and India is largely done on hand-looms. However, the use of the power loom is expanding; this is particularly so in India where the increasing domestic demand for saris is justifying the increased use of this type of loom. Viet Nam continues to develop its silk-weaving industry, mainly on power looms. Practically all weaving in Brazil and the Republic of Korea is carried out on power looms.

Producers of silk fabrics in China and the Republic of Korea are highly dependent on fairly large export orders owing to the size of their production units. According to trade sources, one of the greatest advantages of Indian and Thai exporters is the willingness of their weavers to accept comparatively small orders, enabling the exporters to meet the highly specific requirements of their customers in competitive markets such as Germany.

Because of the special characteristics of hand-loom silk fabrics, it has been essential to educate buyers/importers and, where necessary, consumers as well about the slight variations in colour shades, the unevenness of the weave, etc. that occur in hand-loom weaving. This applies particularly to repeat orders, which will not necessarily fully match the shades of the initial order.

Trade

Textiles and garments

It is difficult to assess the value of the world trade in silk garments and accessories as national trade statistics are either not standardized or not detailed enough. In most countries, for instance, silk garments are normally classified with garments of other fibres such as linen, cashmere and ramie. For the same reason it is practically impossible to find reliable global data on the value of international trade in hand-loomed silk fabrics. Especially in India and Thailand, the most experienced producers of this type of silk fabrics, the majority of silk fabric exports are fabrics woven by hand-looms.

Nonetheless, the international trade in silk textiles and garments can be safely regarded as a multi-billion-dollar affair. During the ISA Congress in Lyon in July 1999, trade sources indicated that in 1998 the United States retail market for silk products was estimated at some US$ 5 billion.

Haute couture creations, by definition, go to a very small clientele; the bulk of the silk trade is directed to other consumer segments. The comparative scarcity of the raw material will have to be kept in mind when developing silk products for these segments of the international market. It may be interesting to note that, according to trade sources, the number of regular *haute couture* clients in the world has declined quite drastically from about 300,000 before the Second World War to only about 1,000 today. In fact, several famous *couture* houses seem to be more successful in marketing perfumes and accessories than clothing. No doubt *haute couture* still maintains an important role in image building, but its overall significance is diminishing. After all, the number of clients who are willing to pay US$ 15,000–25,000 for a dress is somewhat limited. It is estimated that the *haute couture* industry currently employs only about 41,000 individuals.

Sand-washed silk and its effects on trade

During the 1980s, some New York-based entrepreneurs started testing and developing a silk fabric that would be crease-resistant, pre-shrunk and even machine washable. Fabrics were washed in machines with sand, pebbles, tennis balls and even tennis shoes. The end result, a fabric that was very soft, comfortable and, most importantly, easy to maintain (i.e. to wash and iron), was a huge commercial success. Sand-washed silk fit into the 1990s' vogue for elegant, comfortable sports and leisure wear made of natural fibres. Not surprisingly, therefore, imports of sand-washed garments [mainly from China and Hong Kong (China)] into the West soared.

Traditionally, more than 90% of the world market for silk garments was geared to women's wear. Silk products for men were in the past largely limited to shirts, neckties, handkerchiefs, socks and underwear. The situation has changed significantly in the West, a direct result of the marketing of sand-washed silk. There was a wide range of sand-washed silk garments for men: trousers, jackets, padded winter jackets, bomber jackets, shirts, suits, shorts, T-shirts, etc. Some trade sources indicate that sand-washed silk may continue to have a future in men's clothing, but at higher quality and price levels.

The public perception of the right time to use silk garments has also shifted, at least in the traditional European markets. Silk used to be reserved mainly for evening wear, but sand-washed silk has made the use of silk garments possible at any time of the day. Hitherto sold only in high-street boutiques, silk garments and accessories are now available in department stores and from mail-order houses.

Other innovative silk products

During the 1990s, other silk items made in developing countries were successfully launched in several Western markets. An example is thermal underwear from China, which was introduced some years ago in Canada and the United States. This product is sold through specialist shops to skiers, mountain climbers and the like. Its main sales points are the special characteristics of silk, which is cool in summer, warm in winter and absorbs moisture without giving the sensation of wetness.

Knitted silk goods (T-shirts, camisoles, polo-neck sweaters and cardigans) have lately appeared in various European markets and in Japan. Knitted products of silk blended with cotton, linen, acrylic and viscose have been selling well in the middle price categories in Europe and especially in the United States. Luxury fibres such as cashmere, alpaca and camel hair are also blended with silk. There is a growing demand for knitted products both in silk and silk blends. The main suppliers for these products are Italy and China. This goes very well with the present fashion for casual dressing and it is believed that this is the trend for the future in several Western markets.

International suppliers

Raw silk and silk yarn. China is the dominant supplier of raw silk and silk yarn to the West. Many silk-producing developing countries are also heavily dependent on China for their basic supplies. The other main sources, but on a much smaller scale, are Brazil and Viet Nam.

Certain countries use up their own output of raw silk; some of these supplement domestic supplies with imports from China, Brazil and Viet Nam. India is a case in point: it is both the world's second largest producer of raw silk and the biggest importer of this material.

Finished silk goods. The finished silk goods marketed internationally in fairly recent times came mainly from Europe. Today, some developing and other countries/areas produce these goods for export on a large scale. China, India and Thailand are notable examples of comparatively new producers. Hong Kong (China), China and the Republic of Korea have been in the business of exporting large quantities of silk garments to Western markets for longer periods.

China as a supplier. China's silk exports climbed from US$ 1.1 billion in 1986 to US$ 2.9 billion in 1993, then fell to US$ 1.62 billion in 1999. As mentioned earlier, the role of China in international trade in raw silk and silk products has undergone a fundamental change over the last two decades. It had replaced Japan as the world's largest producer of raw silk by 1978, with its share in world output climbing to more than 70% in 1998. Primarily an exporter of raw silk and silk yarn in the past, the share of these materials in its overall silk trade declined from about 33% in 1986 to around 10% today. The country is now mainly an exporter of value-added silk products, with their share in the country's overall silk trade rising from 23% in 1986 to over 70% today. The latter change was brought about by some American buyers who invented sand-washing as a softening treatment for silk fabrics, a treatment, which revolutionized the silk trade.

Imposition of quotas

The rapid increase of sand-washed silk exports from China to the European Union and the United States eventually, and perhaps inevitably, led to quantitative restrictions on both these markets. In the United States the restrictions were imposed after consultations between the two parties. In the European Union, they were imposed unilaterally by the European Commission in March 1994. Fortunately for China and Hong Kong (China), the main suppliers, demand for sand-washed silk garments in the West had already peaked. The quotas, therefore, had somewhat smaller impact than originally anticipated.

It is interesting to note that in these two markets Chinese exports were not considered a threat to the local silk-processing industries. This was particularly so in the United States, which has no domestic silk-processing industry to speak of. The threat arose from the fact that the cheap silk products were competing with products of other fibres, including cotton and even polyester. The quota restrictions in both markets are still in place; in the European Union both for Chinese silk fabrics and garments, in the United States for silk garments only.

It would seem that one of the essential challenges to the silk producers of today is to strike the right balance between the various segments of the market. The appearance of silk as a mass product does not have to mean its disappearance from the middle and higher echelons of the market.

In fact, the increasing pressure in Europe towards the use of environmentally benign products may have a greater impact on international trade. This pressure, particularly strong among consumer groups in Germany, will continue to lead to stringent legislation on both production methods and end products. Legislation banning certain azo-dyes was introduced in Germany (*see* page 12) some five years ago and some other European countries have already (the Netherlands) or can be expected to follow suit. The new European Union criteria introduced in March 1999 for eco-labels for textiles and clothing also ban these azo-dyes.

Consumption

After the sand-washed silk experience, silk consumption in the developed countries seems to have stagnated over the last couple of years. The market is slowly recovering from the 'democratization' of silk and new attractive alternatives for silk consumers are expected. Lately, two new interesting trends have appeared: first, knitted silk goods are increasingly gaining popularity; and second, the demand for blended silk fabrics for garments, both knitted and woven, is on a steady rise (silk blended with linen, cotton, wool, hemp, viscose, cashmere, alpaca, etc.). One reason for the silk demand is probably the popularity of natural fibres, even though it must be mentioned that this aspect has hardly featured in any effort to promote silk products. Another reason is the availability of reasonably priced made-up silk goods, which consumers in the middle-income groups can afford.

Per capita consumption of silk in Europe has traditionally been highest in Switzerland, followed by Germany and the United Kingdom. France and Italy, the two leading silk converters, have always had somewhat lower domestic consumption figures, which seems to indicate that production of silk products in these countries is largely geared towards export markets.

Japan has long traditions in the use of silk and consequently the country has the highest per capita consumption of silk in the world. Although consumption has fallen in recent years, principally because of a drop in demand for kimonos, Japan's position is likely to remain unchanged as demand rises for other silk products. Over the past few years Japan's imports of clothing (including silk items) from China have increased considerably. This is not surprising since the suppliers are close to the market, allowing the Japanese specialists to visit the suppliers frequently. Similar cultural background also facilitates the growth of this bilateral trade. In 1998 Japan was the third largest importer of Chinese silk products, after Hong Kong (China) and the United States, totalling some US$ 280 million.

In India, domestic consumption, at 85% of production, is substantial. No significant rise in export trade will be possible in this country without an accompanying expansion of production. The situation is not expected to change in the near future. India will have to open its doors to competing products of silk and other fibres from external suppliers in the year 2005, when full implementation of the WTO Agreement on Textiles and Clothing (ATC) takes place. It remains to be seen how the Indian silk industry will compete with foreign suppliers of silk and other suitable sari fabrics once the existing very high tariff barriers have to be lowered.

The most recent reports indicate that the domestic demand for silk in China is rapidly increasing with rising standards of living, particularly in the country's coastal belts. The same applies to the Republic of Korea and Viet Nam. In China, however, the impact on the country's export trade (particularly in raw materials and semi-finished products) of rising local demand and the simultaneous falling of raw silk production needs to be carefully scrutinized.

Generic promotion

One of the organizations engaged in the generic promotion of silk is the International Silk Association (ISA) in Lyon, France. With members in about 30 producing and consuming countries, ISA mainly represents the commercial interests of silk industries and traders and is little involved in the development of sericulture. It has introduced the use of a silk mark for fabrics and garments.

Some people in the silk trade believe that activities leading to the development or adoption of a widely recognized silk mark, supported by active promotion, should be carried out as soon as possible. Not only should the mark serve to identify genuine silk products, but it should also act as a guarantee of quality. Research would be essential to determining basic quality specifications for the mark and standardized care instructions should be developed. Furthermore, producers accepting the use of the mark would have to agree to conform strictly to all the standards.

The frequent use of the word 'silk' to describe a variety of products (such as cigarettes, shampoos, beer – 'pure silk in a glass' – and even other textiles) and services (airlines, for example) seems to indicate that silk has properties which when evoked would make other products more saleable. For a period of about 15 years the five major European silk processors had a promotional programme for silk in cooperation with China. This activity came to an end since the

Chinese did not want to continue financing a campaign that did not specifically advertise Chinese silk. However, during the promotion period there were funds available, at least on a modest scale, for trade promotion at some leading retail outlets, such as Harrods in London. Some of the money was also used for press releases and brochures for consumers. In general, however, silk producers and processors do not seem to be convinced that promotional activities for silk itself are required. Nevertheless during the XXIst ISA Congress in November 1997 in Bangkok, a proposal for the generic promotion of silk was tabled by the ISA Promotion Committee.

There have also been occasional country-specific campaigns, such as the 'Silk at Heart' promotion in Japan in the 1980s, but today for all practical purposes no general promotional activity is carried out on silk. This is unfortunate, particularly in view of the damage done to its image by the sand-washed silk boom.

The promotion of silk and silk products is at present left to individual countries and enterprises. While activities on a larger scale have been discussed at international forums for several years, many show interest in such activities as long as they do not have to provide the funds required.

It is obvious that the development of a silk mark and the promotion of the silk trade in general would require cooperation among silk-producing countries, silk converters and traders. A strengthened ISA or similar organization would be required to coordinate activities.

Ecology and silk

Environmental and social issues are widely discussed in international textile and clothing circles. Western European countries, led by Germany, are becoming more and more demanding on such matters as production processes, child labour, social clauses, social labels and the use of dangerous chemicals and dyes. The trade itself has been slowly focusing on environmentally friendly products and production methods. For the time being there are no mandatory rules on eco-labelling, even though a host of eco-labelling schemes exist in many Western markets. In some countries, such as Sweden and Germany, several competing scenarios are available.

Silk has a lot to offer in this respect: it is user-friendly and environmentally sound. Essentially composed of proteins, it is close to the human skin. It can absorb up to 30% of its weight in moisture, making it extremely comfortable to wear. From the point of view of the environment, silk has the advantage of being produced with few chemical fertilizers and practically no insecticides. These environmentally positive aspects have so far hardly featured in any sales campaigns. They should be vigorously used for the benefit of the international trade in silk products.

In March 1999 the European Union issued comprehensive environmental criteria for the use of European Union eco-labels for all textiles and clothing items. It remains to be seen how the manufacturers will react, since the previous European Union eco-label criteria for T-shirts and bed linen attracted only a handful of European manufacturers to apply for the label. It has to be kept in mind that the European Union eco-label is, like all the others, a voluntary label and using the label does not necessarily bring any clear benefit over similar competing (non-labelled) products.

In the Union, the life cycle of industrial products – 'from cradle to grave' – has become a matter of concern and their environmental effects before, during and after production are being subjected to scrutiny. One result is the bewildering array of competing eco-labelling systems created by different organizations with varying objectives in individual European countries.

Germany has perhaps been more active than any other European country on environmental issues. The health of consumers was taken into account by the Federal Ministry of Health's amendment of 15 July 1994 to the *Consumer Goods Ordinance* (which regulates all consumer commodities). The amendment bans the production, import and sale of any consumer goods containing certain azo-dyestuffs which, upon decomposition, produce any of the 20 amines suspected to be carcinogenic (*see* list at the end of this chapter). No garments or items which come into regular contact with the human body may be produced, imported and sold in Germany if they release harmful amines as a result of the use of these azo-dyes. The ban became effective in April 1996. The same rule is now also valid in the Netherlands for garments, bed linen and footwear.

The regulation has had an impact on silk producers and processors whether they operate for the German and Netherlands markets or not. While the free movement of goods within the Union would make it possible for one country to import the banned fabrics and produce garments for re-export to these markets, the German Ministry of Health, for example, can conduct random checks at the retail level to ensure compliance with the law.

Silk producers and exporters in developing countries should keep themselves informed through their business contacts in importing countries on the evolving regulations in their target markets.

The harmful amines covered by the German regulation are listed below:

Amines	*CAS Number**
4-aminodiphenyl	*92-67-1*
Benzidine	*92-87-5*
4-clorotoluidine	*95-69-2*
2-naphthylamine	*91-59-8*
0-aminoazotoluene	*97-56-3*
2-amino-4-nitrotoluene	*99-55-8*
p-chloroaniline	*106-47-8*
2,4-diaminoanisole	*615-05-4*
4,4'-diaminodiphenylmethane	*101-77-9*
3,3'-dichlorobenzidine	*91-94-1*
3,3'-dimethoxybenzidine	*119-90-4*
3,3'-dimethylbenzidine	*119-93-7*
3,3'-dimethyl-4,4'-diaminodiphenylmethane	*838-88-0*
p-kresidine	*120-71-8*
4,4'-methylene-bis-(2-chloraniline)	*101-14-4*
4,4'-oxydianiline	*101-80-4*
4,4'-thiodianiline	*139-65-1*
o-toluidine	*95-53-4*
2,4-toluylenediamine	*95-80-7*
2,4,5-trimethylaniline	*137-17-7*

*** Chemical Abstracts Service Registry Numbers.**

CHAPTER 2

World production and trade

Overview

As has been reported in previous editions of this survey, the world trade in silk and silk products went through a radical change over the last two decades, affecting both sources of supply and the nature of demand on the international market.

As the figures in table 2 have shown, both China and India have overtaken Japan as producers of raw silk. Their outputs in 2000, at 50,683 and 15,214 tons respectively, were far larger than Japan's 557 tons. Japan's industrialization and the high labour cost and land requirements for silkworm rearing have made this traditionally important activity too uneconomic, and the country is now a net importer of raw silk.

China is also today's largest supplier of raw silk to the international market. India, by contrast, has become the world's largest importer of raw silk.

The trade in made-up silk goods, once dominated by Europe, is now increasingly characterized by the presence of developing countries. China is an outstanding example. India has also become a supplier of ready-to-wear garments (mainly for women) and items for interior decoration such as bedspreads and cushion covers. Thailand also exports finished silk goods although this trade has declined in recent years. As in the past, Thailand's exports will continue to depend to some extent on imported supplies of raw silk and silk yarn.

As mentioned earlier, demand for silk fabrics and made-up goods was once restricted to high-cost luxury items for a selected clientele at the upper-income levels. This demand has expanded in recent years to include lower-priced goods within the reach of consumers in the middle-income groups.

Trade sources have stated that the vogue for sand-washed silk has damaged the image of silk. As this vogue peaked, consumers were offered pure silk shirts and blouses at prices significantly lower than those of goods made of cotton, viscose or even polyester. At such low prices, the quality of the garments had to be rather poor. Many traders are of the view that since supplies of raw silk are and are likely to remain limited, it is now in the long-term interest of everyone in the silk trade to keep substandard goods off the market.

The situation has in some cases been aggravated by the incentive policies of some silk-producing countries. These have encouraged silk exporters to sell their products – at any cost and almost at any price. In the end, such policies have damaged relations with international business partners.

One aspect of international trade remains the same: European converters retain their supremacy as finishers of silk. An example is Hermès, the producer par excellence of scarves and neckties for the top end of the market. However, silk traders believe that manufacturers in developing countries will continue to increase their presence on the world market as they improve their technical skills and upgrade their machinery, thereby raising the quality of their products. In effect, there is a clientele for luxury items as well as a demand for products in the lower price categories.

International trade

Participants in the trade

The participants in the international silk trade can be divided into four categories:

- Mainly raw silk producers (Uzbekistan, Viet Nam).
- Raw silk producers and manufacturers of processed silk goods (Brazil, China, India, Thailand and Uzbekistan).
- Silk-converting countries which rely entirely on imported raw materials (France, Germany, Italy, Japan, the Republic of Korea, Switzerland and the United Kingdom).
- Countries which neither produce raw silk nor process it (certain European countries, Australia, New Zealand, Canada, the United States, and most of Africa and Latin America).

Product categories

Imports (and exports) can be divided into two groups: raw silk, silk waste, silk yarn and grey fabrics for further processing; and finished silk fabrics (dyed or printed), ready-made garments, made-up goods, items for interior decoration, etc.

First category. The trade in the first category of products is supplied by China, followed a long way behind by Brazil and Viet Nam. This trade can be said to be characterized by the dependence of almost all converters around the world on raw silk and yarn from China, which supplies about 80% of global imports. According to the China National Silk Import & Export Corporation (CNSIEC), the largest importers of Chinese silk products (all categories) in 1999 were as follows:

Importer	*Imports (US$ '000,000)*	*Change from 1998 (%)*
Hong Kong (China)	644	– 1.6
Japan	313	+12.2
United States	396	–10.6
Republic of Korea	133	+ 1.9
Germany	23	– 4.4
Italy	27	+ 1.5
India	134	+28.5
Total	***1 830***	

Source: CNSIEC, Beijing.

India is now the world's largest importer of raw silk. According to trade estimates, its imports of raw silk from all sources, i.e. China, Brazil, Hong Kong (China) and Viet Nam, reached between 7,000 and 8,000 tons in 1999. Chinese raw silk exports were in 1999 some 7,990 tons, a drop of 5.8% from the corresponding figure in 1998.

Second category. Fabrics belong to the second category of products traded. In analysing the related import figures, one must distinguish between types of fabric. Italy, for instance, imports mainly low-value, grey (loom-state) silk fabrics from China. Exports of silk fabrics from China were reduced by 7.2% from the 1998 figure to 86.9 million metres in 1999. Interestingly, at the same time the exports of Chinese printed or dyed silk fabrics have increased by 49.7% from the 1998 figure up to 14.6 million metres. Exports of silk fabrics from European converters consist only of higher-value finished fabrics, mainly for tailoring.

Hong Kong (China) and China taken together are today the world's largest converters of silk fabrics, mainly into industrially processed garments for men and women. It is therefore not surprising that the share of made-up silk articles in China's overall silk trade has risen steadily in recent years. Its exports of finished silk goods, worth about US$ 380 million in 1989, reached US$ 842 million by 1991, the latter figure including US$ 302 million worth of 100% silk goods. In 1999, its exports of garments and other made-up goods were valued at US$ 852.6 million, 27.6% lower than the 1998 figure. These items accounted for about 50% of China's overall silk exports in 1999.

Hong Kong (China) is the world's leading producer of silk garments. It obtains its raw material mainly from China, which supplied US$ 644 million worth of silk yarn and fabrics in 1999, 1.6% down on the 1998 figure. An estimated 60% of the silk garments produced in Hong Kong (China) are sent to the United States; the balance is exported to various European and other countries.

As there are practically no silk printers and finishers in the United States, most of the fabrics entering this rapidly expanding market are in finished form. Imports into the United States of all woven silk fabrics (SITC 654.1) amounted to US$ 285 million in 2000. The main suppliers among developing countries were China and India.

The value of the trade in finished silk goods cannot be accurately estimated owing to the lack of reliable statistical data. The situation has not been helped by the fact that country-specific data in the European Union became rather meaningless after the creation of the European single market in 1993. Consequently, it has become difficult to determine whether imported silk products are actually consumed in the importing European Union country.

The role of China and other suppliers in the international silk trade

China

China today plays a clearly dominant role in the international silk trade. Announcements by Chinese authorities of new plans and export strategies are studied carefully by the world's silk converters and importers. China currently supplies more than 80% of world imports of raw silk and yarn. In 1999 its exports of raw silk were down to 6,151 tons, a considerable drop from 10,187 tons in 1996. However, its exports of raw silk in 2000 were almost 10,500 tons. It should be noted though that the share of raw silk in China's overall silk trade has been steadily declining over the years, from 49% in 1980 to less than 10% in 1999.

According to statistical data from the Chinese Customs Office China's exports of silk and silk products amounted to US$ 1.62 billion in 1999, down by 17.4% from the corresponding figure in 1998. More than 60% of the 1999 exports consisted of silk fabrics and finished silk goods.

China has been shifting production of exportable silk goods to further processed silk items and has been tackling the challenge of modernizing its silk industry. It has established several joint ventures aiming at improving the quality and finish of fabrics and garments destined for export. Well-known European and United States fashion designers have some of their collections of silk garments produced in China under the supervision and quality control of foreign technicians. Major department store groups, chain stores and mail-order houses in the United States and Europe have also been cooperating closely with the Chinese in the production of silk garments and made-up goods for retail. Lately, many famous Japanese trading houses and department stores have been closely cooperating with Chinese silk producers to develop silk garment collections for the Japanese market.

Until the end of 1993, 100% silk products were given preferential treatment in the United States and the European Union in the form of quota-free access. Most of the other textile fibres fell under the Multifibre Arrangement (MFA) and hence were subject to quota restrictions. In 1994, however, in the wake of the explosive growth in imports of sand-washed silk garments primarily from China and Hong Kong (China), quotas were established for silk garments. The quotas on silk garments in the United States market were negotiated between the two parties. In Europe, the quotas were unilaterally imposed by the European Union and the quotas cover both ready-made garments and finished silk fabrics.

Other suppliers

China's overall domination of the international silk trade will, no doubt, continue for years to come, despite the growing number of aspiring silk producers, such as Bangladesh, Bolivia, Colombia, Côte d'Ivoire, the Islamic Republic of Iran, Paraguay, Peru, Sri Lanka, Turkey and Uganda.

Brazil's output is exported mainly to Japan (73% in 1999) and mostly in the form of raw silk or silk yarn. In the past year and a half, Brazil's A-grade raw silk has been selling at US$ 34–38 a kilogram as against around US$ 20 for the comparable 3A-grade raw silk from China. As Japan is currently importing less raw silk and more finished silk goods, Brazil now supplies the Republic of Korea, France, India and Italy, among other markets. Further efforts will have to be made to deal with the problems arising from its high price levels.

Viet Nam launched in the mid 1980s a substantial rehabilitation programme for its sericulture sector. Its silk output steadily increased from a modest 120 tons in 1987 to 900 tons in 1993 and to 1,500 tons in 1996. Since then, however, the annual raw silk production in Viet Nam has been declining and in 1999 was some 780 tons only. Viet Nam also has to overcome the marketing difficulties posed by the low prices of Chinese silk. Over time, the country's long history of sericulture and silk production should help it to develop into a significant supply source for silk processors. Furthermore, its silk-weaving industry hopes to attain quality levels that will enable domestic garment producers to use local fabrics in the manufacture of garments for export for a higher local content.

Demand for raw silk in silk-producing countries

Unlike other textile fibres, silk is largely consumed in the silk-producing developing countries, which have their domestic markets as their main outlets. India, for example, uses most of its output of raw silk. The expansion of exports of silk products from this country continues to be directly linked to increased production of raw silk or to a growth in imports. In the current world supply situation, imports of raw silk and silk yarn will have to come primarily from China. Some of India's leading exporters of high quality silk goods depend entirely on imports for their raw materials.

The latest reports indicate that silk consumption in Japan is reviving and stabilizing. One reason is the surge in interest in Western garments and accessories made of silk. Despite the decline in the use of kimonos, the main contributor to the fall in recent years of silk consumption in Japan, kimonos continue to absorb a vast majority of the silk available in the country.

Recent statements by Chinese officials indicate that demand in China for silk is on the upswing because of improving standards of living. Consumption trends in the Republic of Korea appear to be similar to those in Japan. Here, too, the drop in the use of the national costume has been accompanied by the increasing popularity of Western-style clothes.

It is important to keep domestic consumption levels in silk-producing countries in mind when making projections for the international silk trade. A balance should be sought between producing for the more lucrative export markets and producing for expanding domestic markets. It may be noted that in 1999 Chinese silk exports to several countries in the region were far higher than the year before: Japan (40%), Republic of Korea (31.4%), India (52.3%) and Singapore, Malaysia and Thailand (12.4%). There has been a significant increase in exports of dyed and printed fabrics from China to the South and South East Asian region, including printed habutai and other lightweight silk fabrics.

CHAPTER 3

The promotion of silk

Generic promotion

In Europe, silk was promoted generically between the early 1970s and 1989 by the European Commission for the Promotion of Silk (Commission européenne pour la promotion de la soie, or CEPS), which conducted its activities in France, Germany, Italy, Switzerland and the United Kingdom. Financing was provided through a 'levy' on raw silk purchases from China. These funds were allocated to each country on the basis of silk imports from China and the size of the market.

CEPS promoted silk through publicity campaigns, by advertising in fashion magazines and by publishing educational materials on silk for distribution in schools and similar places. There is no doubt that the Commission, in its 15 years of operation, contributed to the growth of awareness of silk and silk products among consumers in its member countries.

Trade sources indicate that there remains a great need for information campaigns among consumers in both Europe and the United States. They point out that promotional activities for silk have been insignificant compared with activities carried out for linen, cotton and wool. At the XXIst ISA Congress, held in Bangkok in November 1997, the ISA Promotion Committee tabled a proposal to generate funds for the generic promotion of silk.

A silk mark, similar to the wool mark or the cotton emblem, should be strongly promoted to facilitate recognition of silk products and as a guarantee of quality in retail shops. Realistic and standardized care instructions should be developed and disseminated widely. The use of the 'L' symbol to promote linen may be a suitable example for the silk industry to emulate. Linen, in fact, has been very successfully promoted over the past 15 years by the European Union and a number of European producers and processors. When the promotion for linen was started in the mid 1980s linen was primarily used for home textiles, such as kitchen towels, table cloths and napkins. Lately, linen has been mainly used for clothing, both in 100% linen and in a variety of blends, such as cotton/linen, silk/linen, viscose/linen. It goes without saying, however, that considerable funds have been allocated for the linen promotion over the years.

Special effort should be devoted to disseminating information on the special characteristics of hand-loom products, even among retailers. The uneven weave and the difficulty of obtaining matching colours in repeat orders are aspects of hand-loom silks that should be highlighted in information campaigns.

In order to promote silk products from Asia, the United Nations Economic and Social Commission for Asia and the Pacific organized five Asian International Silk Fairs between 1984 and 1992. Two were held in Hong Kong (China) (1984 and 1986), one in Amsterdam (1988) and one in Munich (1990). The fifth was held in connection with the IGEDO Fair in Düsseldorf in September 1992. Unfortunately, this activity has been discontinued, at least for the time being.

Additionally, several silk-producing countries display their collections regularly at international trade fairs such as Heimtextil in Frankfurt and IGEDO in Düsseldorf.

On various occasions, representatives of silk-producing developing and consuming countries have expressed their interest in the creation of a universally accepted silk mark, which would benefit both silk producers and end-users. The interest of European silk converters in such a mark has been somewhat lukewarm.

It should be noted that major silk producers and exporters such as China, India and Thailand also promote their silk goods as distinctly national products.

The XXIInd Congress of the International Silk Association was held in Lyon, France in July 1999. The Congress was also celebrating the fiftieth anniversary of the association. The repositioning of silk was discussed at length during the Congress. The aftermath of the sand-washed silk boom was still being felt and the raw silk price (3A grade) was at the time about US$ 20 a kilogram, compared to the corresponding price in 1989 of US$ 50 a kilogram.

Global information system on silk

In various forums in developing and developed countries, the need for transparent information on production, trade flows, demand trends, prices, fashion trends, exporters' and importers' registers at an international level has repeatedly been stressed. Some countries, notably India and China, have efficient national information systems. In the developed countries, particularly at the trade association level and in individual enterprises, valuable quantitative and qualitative information of a non-confidential nature is available.

It had long been felt that an efficient information system would also contribute to the development of overall awareness of silk and as well as to silk promotion efforts. Today the need for the system is even more self-evident in view of the continuing confusion, first alluded to in this survey in 1995, among textile and garment producers in developing countries about international trading conditions. The WTO Agreement on Textiles and Clothing (ATC), and the implementation or planned implementation of market regulations on production methods, eco-labelling, child labour, social clauses, social labels, the use of chemicals and dyes, and the disposal of consumer goods have made it difficult for individual enterprises and even entire countries to grasp the requirements of their target markets, as well as the trade opportunities these changes represent. An information system covering these matters would go a long way towards eliminating this confusion.

Since August 1995, ITC has been organizing technical workshops on ATC and its possible implications for developing countries and economies in transition. So far some 2,500 industry leaders and government officials in various parts of the world have attended these workshops.

Workshop material can be found on ITC's official website (*www.intracen.org*), including indication of changes that are taking place or may take place during the transition period provided for by the ATC. This transition period will end on 31 December 2004. As mentioned earlier, after that date the trade in textiles and clothing will fall under the common WTO rules for trade in goods. The website provides coverage of interest also to silk producers, processors and traders in many parts of the world.

CHAPTER 4

Consumer markets

Western Europe

While the import statistics provided in this section cannot be said to be complete, they cover a large proportion of the trade and are useful indicators of general trends.

France, Germany, Italy, Switzerland and the United Kingdom are Europe's leading converters and consumers of silk. Although domestic consumption in each of these countries is fairly substantial, their silk industries are largely geared to the export trade.

Imports

Raw silk. Over the past few years raw silk imports into the European Union have been fluctuating: in 1994 raw silk imports reached 4,415 tons, in 1996 3,284 tons and in 1999 3,028 tons. It is not surprising that the processing of raw silk in Europe has lately decreased, since China, traditionally the raw material supplier to developed countries, is increasingly processing silk into finished products. At the same time, China remains the largest supplier of silk yarn: 3,944 tons in1994, 2,985 tons in 1996, and 2,769 tons in 1999. The second largest supplier has been Brazil, which supplied 417 tons in 1994 and 211 tons in 1999. China's dominance as a supplier is clear: despite the drop in supplies from this source, its share remains over 90%.

Table 3 European Union: major importers of raw silk, 1996–2000 (in tons)

	1996	1999	2000
Total of which:	**3 284**	**3 028**	**3 635**
Italy	2 764	2 727	3 136
France	478	224	318
United Kingdom	25	47	22

Source: ISA.

Italy remained by far the largest single importer of raw silk in the European Union. Recovering from a generally declining trend, its imports in 1999 rose to 2,727 tons, 10% higher than in 1998. In 2000 Italy imported 3,136 tons of raw silk, of which 2,175 tons came from China and 934 tons from Germany. As there is no sericulture in Germany it is evident that German export figures actually refer to re-exports of Chinese raw silk into Italy. Ever since the

European Union single market was established in 1993, goods imported into one European Union country may be freely transported to another member country. France imported 224 tons of raw silk in 1999, of which 111 tons came from China and 113 tons from Brazil.

Silk fabrics

Italy is also the EU's leading importer of 100% silk fabrics: in 1997 Italy imported some 2,083 tons of silk fabrics, i.e. more than 70% of the EU total that year. In 1999 the corresponding figures were 1,166 tons or some 40% of the total EU imports, as indicated in table 4.

Table 4 European Union: imports of silk fabrics, 1997–2000 (in tons)

Destination	1997	1999	2000
Total of which:	**2 616**	**2 713**	**3 286**
Italy	2 083	1 166	1 505

Source: ISA.

Silk garments

EU imports of silk dresses, blouses, scarves and neckties in the years 1994, 1996, 1998 and 2000 are shown in tables 5–8. The figures clearly reveal that there was a considerable boom, particularly in imports of silk blouses, during the sand-washed silk period in 1994.

Table 5 European Union: imports of silk dresses, 1994–2000 (in tons)

Source	1994	1996	1998	2000
Total of which:	**555**	**508**	**422**	**826**
China	355	332	245	653
India	75	88	99	94

Source: ISA.

The import figures for ladies' silk dresses did not fluctuate greatly during the second half of the 1990s, but the figure for 2000 shows a clear upswing. The import figures for silk blouses show the impact of the sand-washed silk boom: in 1994 the EU imported 4,375 tons of silk blouses but six years later in 2000 the imports were down to just 1,277 tons. In each case the share of Chinese silk blouses was more than 60% of the total. The import figures for silk scarves indicate that India's market share in the EU is gradually increasing: in 1994, out of total imports of 810 tons, China's share was 433 tons and India's 174 tons, or 21.5%. In 2000 total imports were 802 tons, out of which 330 tons came from China and 213 tons, or 26.6%, came from India. Imports of silk neckties into the EU have been steadily growing: in 1994 392 tons of neckties were imported, out of which 183 tons came from China. The second largest supplier was the Republic of Korea with 55 tons. In 2000 altogether 775 tons of ties were imported; 335 tons came from China and 94 tons from the Republic of Korea.

It is interesting to note that the EU has become the biggest importer of Indian mulberry silk goods: in 1999/2000 the EU took around 53% of Indian silk garment supplies, compared to 43.3% a year earlier.

Table 6 European Union: imports of silk blouses, 1994–2000 (in tons)

Source	1994	1996	1998	2000
Total of which:	**4 375**	**2 138**	**1 372**	**1 277**
China	3 675	1 770	1 372	1 046
India	88	68	66	55

Source: ISA.

Table 7 European Union: imports of silk scarves, 1994–2000 (in tons)

Source	1994	1996	1998	2000
Total of which:	**810**	**864**	**660**	**802**
China	433	407	342	330
India	174	174	119	213
Republic of Korea	30	68	49	80
Madagascar	46	65	49	43

Source: ISA.

Table 8 European Union: imports of silk neckties, 1994–2000 (in tons)

Source	1994	1996	1998	2000
Total of which:	**392**	**397**	**464**	**775**
China	183	124	151	335
Republic of Korea	55	83	71	94
Slovakia	17	59	57	85
Viet Nam	1	1	21	55
Switzerland	40	44	28	44

Source: ISA.

Exports

Silk processing in Europe is concentrated in Milan and Como in Italy. Other centres are Lyon in France, and Zurich in Switzerland; some high-quality silk weaving (jacquard) and printing is undertaken in the United Kingdom.

Italy is traditionally by far the most important supplier of finished silk and mixed silk fabrics (dyed/printed) and in 1998 the country exported some 2,386 tons of silk fabrics. This dropped to 1,985 tons in 1999 before recovering slightly to 2,135 tons in 2000.

The leading European exporters have a reputation for high-quality, fashionable and exclusive silk goods. Italy and France specialize in designer fabrics and scarves from famous fashion houses. British exporters are known for their materials for neckties, both printed and jacquard-woven. The present fashion in neckties favours jacquard-woven ties, after a long fashion period of printed ties. Even so there is always demand for high quality printed neckties, such as Hermès in France.

Other developments

Trade with the United States. In September 1995, the United States Customs Department issued new rules in regard to the determination of the country of origin of imports of textiles and apparel. The new rules became effective on 1 July 1996. In general the rules designate the location where 'the most important assembly or manufacturing' or where the 'last important assembly or manufacturing' has taken place as country of origin.

For the textile trade, this meant that, for United States customs purposes, the country of origin is the place where the grey or loom-state fabric is woven. For the silk printing and dyeing industry in Europe, which imports most of its grey silk fabrics from China, this implied that most of its exports to the United States of finished fabrics would be regarded as having originated in China.

This rule was contested by the European Union at the WTO in May 1997. The EU alleged that the United States had introduced changes to its rules of origin for textile and apparel products which affect exports of EU fabrics, scarves and other flat textile products. As a result, EU products were no longer recognized in the United States as being of EU origin and therefore lost the free access to the United States market that they had hitherto enjoyed. The EU contended that the changes in the rules of origin were in violation of Articles 2.4, 4.2 and 4.4 of the ATC, Article 4.2 of the Agreement on Rules of Origin, Article III of GATT 1994, and Article 2 of the Agreement on Technical Barriers to Trade. In July 1997, United States and EU negotiators reached a tentative agreement effecting a partial rolling back of the 1996 rule. Under the agreement, the United States would exempt silk fabric and scarves imported from Europe from marking requirements that would identify them as a product of China.

Trade with China. Whether the growth in imports of low-cost silk goods was beneficial or not, the image of silk was the subject of debate, with some believing that this image was tarnished as a consequence. However, the inflow of low-cost silk items did encourage first-time buying of silk garments. It remains to be seen whether these new consumers will continue to buy silk.

One rather drastic effect of the upswing in imports of finished silk articles was the unilateral imposition of quotas on Chinese silk garments, accessories and finished fabrics by the European Union in 1994. This action followed lobbying by some European silk processors. Until 1994, silk was one of the very few non-restricted textile materials in international trade. The imposition of quotas caused some disquiet. As quotas are normally imposed to protect domestic industries, the absence of a competing European silk industry (at the level of the products concerned) made the EU quotas a subject of even greater controversy.

However, despite the quotas which have been in place since 1994, Chinese suppliers of garments have still been dominating the EU market.

France

France has remained one of the important European silk processors, together with Italy and Switzerland. For centuries, the French city of Lyon has been producing silk fabrics of the highest quality for domestic consumption and for export. The famous fashion houses of Paris and other fashion centres have been, and continue to be, among the city's most important customers.

The French silk industry has been rather badly hit by the decline of the use of silk for *haute couture*, which has been an important niche market for the French silk industry. The steadily decreasing number of consumers able to afford to pay US$ 15,000–20,000 for one dress has made the high-fashion industry much less lucrative than in the past.

More than 70% of the silk fabric on the market has traditionally gone into the production of clothing. There are, however, signs that silk may have a growing market as a material for interior decoration (for use as curtains, wall covers, bedspreads and upholstery). This trend has not remained unnoticed by ISA, which some years ago established a subcommittee on silk used in interior decoration.

International trade

While in the past the French weaving industry could rely on some domestic supplies of raw silk, today it is entirely dependent on imports. As mentioned earlier, in 1999 France imported 224 tons of raw silk, of which 113 tons was from Brazil and the rest from China.

Over the past few years the number of silk weavers in France has been declining, and imports of grège fabrics have been increasing. Hermès, however, continues to weave all of its silk fabrics in Europe.

According to ISA, French silk fabric imports in 1999 were about 295 tons, consisting of a variety of fabrics, both loom-state and finished, such as crêpe, pongee, habutai and shantung. Major suppliers included both India (about 132 tons) and China (about 98 tons).

During the ISA Congress in Lyon in July 1999 the Institut français de la mode presented the findings of a study about the role of silk in the year 2005. Some of the findings were as follows:

Silk is being offered in different exclusive areas, such as:

- Heritage silk: the kimono, the sari, printed and signed scarves, designer garments and accessories; these articles are often based on certain brands, which also have a kind of 'heritage' status.
- Pleasure silk: the products, which the consumer wears for himself or herself, combining pleasure, comfort and practicality. The 'feel-good' syndrome. This silk, in the form of knitwear, may also appeal to men, especially in the United States.

The image of silk has suffered from the sand-washed silk syndrome. During the boom many new customers could afford to buy silk articles. Unfortunately, the poor quality and workmanship of these products disappointed many customers. It may be mentioned here, however, that it was primarily the United States and European buyers of sand-washed silk who were mainly responsible for its relatively poor quality, since the Asian suppliers were simply following the quality instructions of the buyers.

Some of the most promising directions for re-positioning of silk:

- To return to creativity;
- To put silk into everyday life and make it easier to use (easy care);
- To offer a versatile silk adapted to a variety of circumstances (silk blends, knits);
- To recover silk's original mythical and cultural dimensions.

The study was conducted in the United States, Japan, China and the United Kingdom early in 1999.

Germany

With a population of 80 million inhabitants, Germany is by far Europe's largest market for textiles and clothing, including silk products. It has also become one the world's most competitive markets in the sector, and successful penetration of this market would be considered a good reference for any supplier.

The German consumer favours natural fibres, and the current ecological trend in the country will strengthen this demand. Germany is perhaps the most advanced market for environmentally friendly products and production methods. This is well highlighted by the Federal Ministry of Health's amendment of 15 July 1994 to the *Consumer Goods Ordinance* (which regulates all consumer commodities). The amendment, which came into effect in April 1996, bans the production, import and sale of any consumer goods containing certain azo-dyestuffs that, upon decomposition, produce any of the 20 amines suspected to be carcinogenic. (*See* chapter 1 for a list of these amines.) Unlike eco-labelling schemes, which are voluntary, compliance with the legislation on azo-dyes is mandatory. Trade interviews in Germany indicate that in general the suppliers of silk fabrics in developing countries seem to have found ways of avoiding the use of the banned substances.

The country imports large quantities of finished silk products, including clothing, finished silk fabrics and home furnishings. Generally speaking, the market is large enough to absorb lower-priced silk products for mass consumption as well as a significant volume of high-quality silk garments and interior decoration items for a more discerning clientele. In 1999/2000 Germany was the second largest (after the United States) individual importer of mulberry silk goods from India, receiving around 18.5% of all Indian supplies. This was an increase of around 29.2% from the previous year's figure. The same year Germany was the largest importer of Indian tasar silk products.

A fair volume of Germany's imports of silk garments is re-exported to other EU markets, such as France and Italy. In 2000 Germany exported more than 900 tons of raw silk to Italy. This is mainly re-exports of Chinese raw silk, since there is no production of raw silk in Germany. According to ISA, Germany also imported in 1999 some 1,179 tons of silk waste from China – mainly for re-exports to Italy. In 1999 Germany imported a variety of silk fabrics, both semi-finished and finished – some 360 tons, mainly from China (174 tons) and India (141 tons). Germany has traditionally been a good market, particularly for hand-loomed silk products from India, and this trend seems to continue.

Germany has also been a good market for silk items for interior decoration. Over the last decade or so, it has been a large market for silk cushion covers, bedspreads and curtains and demand continues to present opportunities for developing country suppliers. Interior decorators use silk curtain fabrics and wall coverings, in addition to the usual bedspreads and cushions, to create a 'total' look.

German consumers are probably more quality conscious than their counterparts in other European markets. This means that consumers may be more inclined to pay higher prices for a good-quality garment than to buy cheap (substandard) silk products. The traditional German saying 'if it is cheap it cannot be good' still prevails. It is important for first-time silk buyers to be encouraged by the quality of their purchases to continue to buy silk products in the future.

Italy

Italy has traditionally been an important buyer of silk raw materials as well as a processor of quality silk products. The Italian silk-processing industry is located mainly in the north, in the Milan and Como areas. The industry has many family enterprises, which have been modernizing production units to meet increasingly sophisticated demand. The industry has always been strongly export-oriented. Como's silk industry is particularly dependent on exports: about two-thirds of the production is exported.

Knitted goods have been especially important to Italy's production and export trade. The country has over the years been the world's largest importer of waste silk, which is spun into yarn for the production of knitwear. It has always been at the forefront of new trends in the use of silk and silk blends in knitted goods, including the use of lycra with silk.

Domestic production and international trade

Production. Italy's overall production of silk yarn was estimated in 1999 at about 1,970 tons, 8.9% less than in the previous year. Production of silk fabrics in 1999 reached 3,200 tons, about 4% less than in 1998.

Imports. In 1999, imports of raw silk reached 2,727 tons, almost 10% up from imports in 1998. The trend continued in 2000 when raw silk imports reached 3,136 tons, a further increase of around 13%. Imports of silk waste in 1999 were some 2,300 tons, well above the 1998 figure of 1,663 tons. In 2000 the corresponding figure was 2,729 tons. Imports of thrown silk (yarn) were 1,078 tons in 1999, about 20% more than in 1998. Imports of pure silk fabrics in that year amounted to 1,166 tons and in the year 2000 to some 1,505 tons. Imports of ladies blouses amounted to 382 tons in 1999, an increase of more than 15% from the previous year.

Exports. Italy exported a total of 1,421 tons of silk fabrics in 1999, down 20% from the figures for 1998. Some 1,242 tons of men's neckties were exported in 1999.

Italy's silk products have a clear pre-eminence in certain segments of the United States import trade. In 1998 Italy exported some 537 tons of silk fabrics. The corresponding figures for 1999 and 2000 were 482 and 434 tons respectively, showing a clear decline in Italian silk fabric exports. Italy's share of American imports of silk fabrics was about 24% in 1999, the third largest supplier after China and India (both 26% of the market). As far as silk fabrics for neckties are concerned, printed fabrics suffered a loss of around 31% in the year 2000 compared with the corresponding figure of 1999. At the same time there was an increase of 11.4% in demand for yarn-dyed fabrics.

United Kingdom

The small silk-processing industry in the United Kingdom has been diminishing in size over the years, but its jacquard weavers and printers continue to produce high-quality products. Preferences in neckties have moved back to jacquard fabrics after the long dominance of printed ties, giving a boost to British silk weavers.

Unlike the French, German and Italian markets, the British market has a limited demand for high-priced luxury goods; these goods are retailed in the leading luxury stores. The mass market is controlled by the large retail chains, which have a reputation for selling reasonably priced products of good quality. The retail chains have a large influence on consumer behaviour in the United Kingdom.

The British market has over recent years been showing some interest in silk fabrics for interior decoration. This product group continues to have growth potential in several European markets. The United Kingdom has been one of the largest recipients of Indian silk products. In the silk year 1999/2000 the United Kingdom was the third largest market (after the United States and Germany) for Indian mulberry silk goods, with a market share of 12.7% and showing an increase of some 16% over the figure for the previous silk year.

Towards the end of 1989, the Silk Association of Great Britain (SAGB) launched a silk label based on the ISA silk mark. The labels are sold to SAGB members for use on their silk products. The label is not a quality guarantee, but it gives the consumer some information on the special characteristics of silk products. It is intended only for products that are 100% silk.

Switzerland

Although it is a small country, Switzerland plays a significant role in the European silk trade. Switzerland has been traditionally involved with the European silk trade and in the past Swiss silk traders have operated as silk merchants and as silk processors for the luxury end of the market.

In recent years, however, silk processing in Switzerland has been suffering from high manufacturing costs and the fact that the country does not belong to the European Union. There has also been some movement away from silk into competing fibres.

Silk weaving in Switzerland is concentrating, perhaps more than ever before, on small orders from *haute couture* houses. Higher production costs make it very difficult for the Swiss to compete with weavers in Italy and France. In 1999 Switzerland exported 76 tons of silk fabrics to the European Union, 25 tons to Italy, 9 tons to France and 3 tons to the United Kingdom.

Switzerland, not being an EU member, is not subject to EU quota restrictions on Chinese silk products.

Japan

Japan has always been the world's largest consumer of silk, despite the fall in yearly consumption levels from 30,000 tons in the 1960s to 20,700 tons in the early 1990s. In 2000 Japan produced 1,244 tons of cocoons, which was 20% less than in 1999. Domestic raw silk production has been falling over the years, from 20,160 tons in 1975 to 2,250 tons in 1996, and even further to 556 tons in 2000.

In 1965, there were 399,000 cocoon farmers in Japan; by 1996, this number had dropped to 7,900, down 44% from the previous year. In 2000 this figure was just 3,200 farming households. This decline has been due to the fall in the number of sericultural farm households, aging sericultural workers, the lack of workers willing to take their place, and the decline of comparative earnings.

Future cocoon growing in Japan will be carried out by an ever-declining number of cocoon farmers. Automation will increase. The growers working on mountain farms cannot adopt large-scale farming though they will continue to require a cash crop. As a result, the cost of cocoon production will remain high, despite the use of labour-saving devices, and the raw silk from these cocoons will not be able to compete with imports. The survival therefore of the Japanese cocoon grower will depend on the development of new breeds of silk worm producing raw silk of a quality superior to imports and suitable for high-priced products such as kimonos.

Kimonos now absorb less than 50% of Japan's supply of raw silk, down from 90% in the 1970s. Imports of finished silk goods, mainly Western type clothing and accessories, made up about 53% of the country's total silk supply in 1996. This trend still continues.

Imports

Cocoons, raw silk and silk yarn. Imports of dry cocoons reached 1,004 tons in 1998; two years later, in 2000, imports were only 675 tons. Raw silk imports have been steadily growing and in 2000 reached 2,297 tons. Imports of this product category have not fluctuated significantly, remaining at the level of 1,600–2,200 tons in recent years. Imports originate predominantly from China (more than 70% of the total in 2000), with whom Japan has an annual bilateral import agreement, followed by Brazil (about 28% of the total). In 2000 Japan imported 343 tons of silk yarn from Brazil and 826 tons from China. It may be interesting to note that Viet Nam supplied 375 tons of silk yarn to Japan in 2000, a considerable increase from 195 tons in 1999.

China is by far the most important supplier of raw silk and other silk products. This is due to the geographical proximity of the two countries and the ease with which Japan can send its technical experts to China to advise suppliers on quality standards.

Imports of silk yarns have been a little erratic in recent years. From their 1989 level of 1,333 tons, they dropped to 951 tons in 1990, then swung up to 1,737 tons in 1991, 2,291 tons in 1993 and 2,935 tons in 1996. In 2000 silk yarn imports were about 1,909 tons, an increase of almost 250 tons from the previous year. The suppliers were mainly China (826 tons), the Republic of Korea (187 tons), Brazil (343 tons), Viet Nam (375 tons) and Italy (114 tons).

The level of imports of silk fabrics has been steady. In 1996, they reached 25.5 million m^2 compared with 21.6 million m^2 in 1989. In 2000 the corresponding figure was some 14.2 million m^2. There were not very many changes in supply sources, although there were variations in their performances. In 2000 the major silk fabric suppliers were: China (8.5 million m^2) followed by Taiwan Province (China) (1.9 million m^2), the Republic of Korea (1.7 million m^2), Italy (1.0 million m^2) and India (478,000 m^2).

Imports of silk fabrics from China are subject to quantitative restrictions and the importers are allocated import quotas according to their past performance. Imports of silk fabrics from other countries are quota-free. Demand for blended silk fabrics is not significant.

Manufactured silk goods: consumption and imports. Since the early 1990s, Japanese consumers have become more price conscious. China has become Japan's largest supplier of manufactured silk goods and its share in total supplies continues to rise.

The market for manufactured silk goods is dominated by Asian suppliers. In 1995 China accounted for 78% of the value of Japanese imports of manufactured silk products from Asia, as against 64% in 1993. In addition to China, the following Asian countries/areas supply Japan with silk goods: Republic of Korea, Hong Kong (China), Macao (China), Singapore and Taiwan Province (China). As newcomers Viet Nam and India are just beginning to appear in Japan's silk import statistics.

Table 9 Japan: imports of raw silk and silk products, 1999–2000 (in tons)

Product	1999	2000
Total of which:	**13 876**	**15 366**
Raw silk	2 442	2 298
Silk yarn	1 661	1 910
Silk fabrics	1 489	1 383
Finished products of which:	8 284	9 775
Ladies' blouses	*236*	*255*
Scarves	*131*	*216*
Neckties	*1 054*	*1 345*

Source: ISA.

Manufactured silk goods are now sold by Japanese supermarkets and mail-order houses. Silk blouses are the most important items. Knitted silk products have a small market share.

China's domination of the Japanese market for silk goods can be attributed to the following conditions:

- Labour in China is relatively cheap and it is capable of meeting Japanese quality requirements.
- Cultural and linguistic similarities facilitate mutual understanding between business partners.
- Because China is nearby, it is easy for Japanese companies to send their technicians and foremen to control the production process in Chinese factories.

- Foreign investment in China has become attractive to Japanese companies, which have been establishing joint-venture operations in the silk sector since 1994.
- Deliveries are generally quick and reliable.
- China has the technical skills required for embroidering kimonos.

No other country can match China on the above points.

United States of America

Overview

The United States is among the world leaders in silk consumption, with imports valued at well above US$ 2 billion. The large majority of these imports originate from China and Hong Kong (China), which together supply more than 70% of the total, followed by Italy (12%), India (4%) and the Republic of Korea.

Women's and men's apparel make up about 90% of the country's imports of silk goods. The share of women's apparel in total imports of silk apparel is around 70%.

The value of silk goods imported into the United States for home furnishing purposes is between US$ 200 million and US$ 250 million. Trends in home decoration have tended to follow trends in designer apparel. There seems to be a growing demand for silk bedding (e.g. bed sheets, pillowcases, duvet covers, bed covers) at the luxury end of the market. Sales of these items in 1996 were around 15% higher than in the previous year.

As in Europe, the sand-washed silk boom almost destroyed the market for silk as a luxury fabric. In effect, silk was being offered as just another cheap fabric option.

However, sand-washed silk has radically changed the American perception of silk as a fibre only for the affluent. As a consequence, consumers are less likely to be prepared to pay any premium for silk apparel and silk will have to compete with a large variety of other fibres in each price category.

In the apparel sector, American consumers are constantly being offered new types of silk fabrics, imported to a large extent from Italy and China.

- Knitted silk. There is traditional and strong demand for knitted items in many product categories, such as T-shirts, sweaters, skirts and jackets. Silk is now blended with lycra for stretch, as well as with other luxury fibres such as linen or cashmere.
- Fabrics of silk blended with cotton, linen and viscose; blends with stretch fibres in such products as stretch velvet, stretch lace and even stretch denim.

The increasing numbers of working women in the United States have created a strong preference for easy-care products. Garments that have to be dry-cleaned (particularly those in the moderate price categories) are not popular: a dry-cleaning bill of US$ 10 for a US$ 29 silk blouse does not attract customers. For this reason, silk products are facing stiff competition from non-silk garments that are attractive, affordable and washable. Many of these are produced either in the United States or in Mexico, reducing the risk of delays in deliveries to retail outlets.

Trade sources indicate that the steady relaxation of the dress code in the United States office environment is boosting the development of smart casual apparel for office wear. The previous 'casual Friday' has now become the whole working week in many companies. At the same time the number of people working from home is also increasing in the United States.

Imports

Raw silk and silk yarn. Imports of raw silk in 1999 were some 20 tons, about 50% more than in 1998. Silk yarn imports reached 103 tons in 1999, an increase of 11% from the previous year. The low level of imports is not surprising, as the country does not have silk-processing facilities to speak of.

Silk fabrics. The volume of imports of silk fabrics has fluctuated slightly over the last few years. In 1999 Italy was again one of the leading suppliers, its 482 tons or 24% of the silk fabric imports into the United States making it the third largest supplier after China and India (both 26% of the total silk fabric imports). In 2000 silk fabric imports from Italy dropped to 434 tons. India, China and Italy account for 76% of all imports of silk fabrics. It is interesting to note that these three market leaders have lately surpassed the Republic of Korea, which was the market leader only some five years ago.

Table 10 United States: imports of silk and silk products, 1998–2000 (in millions of United States dollars)

	1998	1999	2000
Total of which:	**2 001.3**	**1 980.7**	**2 235.2**
Raw silk/silk yarn	6.6	6.3	5.6
Silk fabrics	288.4	259.4	284.9
Silk garments	1 431.8	1 437.9	1 629.2
Neckties, scarves	171.4	157.1	160.4
Knitted silk products (underwear, sweaters)	103.1	120.0	155.1

Source: ISA.

Apparel and apparel-related products. This product category has had a share of 90% in all silk imports in recent years. According to conservative trade estimates, the retail value of silk apparel in the United States market is some US$ 5 billion–US$ 6 billion.

China has been the largest supplier of silk apparel, with a share of more than 60% across product categories in recent years. Five countries/areas accounted for 90% of all silk goods imported into the country.

Table 11 United States: imports of silk and silk products from China, 1998–2000 (in millions of United States dollars)

	1998	1999	2000
Total of which:	**1 435.7**	**1 431.4**	**1 608.8**
Raw silk/silk yarn	3.2	2.9	1.6
Silk fabrics	68.8	63.3	56.6
Silk garments	1 235.2	1 239.5	1 393.6
Neckties, scarves	22.1	24.2	26.4
Knitted silk products (underwear, sweaters)	86.5	101.6	130.7
% of total imports	*71.7*	*72.3*	*72.0*

Source: ISA.

Table 12 United States: imports of silk and silk products from India, 1998–2000 (in millions of United States dollars)

	1998	1999	2000
Total of which:	**97.9**	**114.9**	**165.6**
Raw silk/silk yarn	0.1	0.1	0.2
Silk fabrics	54.3	67.3	97.7
Silk garments	36.8	40.1	56.5
Neckties, scarves	1.8	2.7	4.2
Knitted silk products (underwear, sweaters)	4.9	4.6	7.0
% of total imports	*4.9*	*5.8*	*7.4*

Source: ISA.

Table 13 United States: imports of silk and silk products from Italy, 1998–2000 (in millions of United States dollars)

	1998	1999	2000
Total of which:	**219.5**	**199.4**	**203.1**
Raw silk/silk yarn	0.8	0.6	0.9
Silk fabrics	77.4	67.6	61.2
Silk garments	46.3	42.5	56.6
Neckties, scarves	90.2	83.3	77.5
Knitted silk products (underwear, sweaters)	4.7	5.4	6.9
% of total imports	*11.0*	*10.1*	*9.1*

Source: ISA.

As has been discussed in chapter 1 of this survey, the rapid growth of imports in the early 1990s led to the unavoidable imposition of quantitative restrictions on Chinese silk apparel in 1994. Despite the quota restrictions, China retains its dominant market position.

United Arab Emirates

The United Arab Emirates (UAE) has developed into a significant market for silk products, especially silk fabrics and saris. As in all member countries of the Gulf Cooperation Council, duty rates are low and the Emirates has a long history of trade with countries in the Gulf as well as with East Africa. The country re-exports an estimated 80% of all its imported goods to markets in the region, including Iraq and the Islamic Republic of Iran. While this does not apply to silk products, which in the main are absorbed by the domestic market, the Emirates re-exports some quantities to Bahrain, Kuwait and Qatar, since these markets are generally too small to import directly the required minimum volumes from silk producers in various parts of the world.

Dubai is the centre of the re-export trade. It is also a centre for sales to tourists from the Russian Federation and Eastern Europe. Among the most popular products are home electronics, gold, clothing and textiles, including silk fabrics.

The Emirates is a natural market for saris from India, since about half its population of 1.6 million people are of Indian origin. It is customary for Indian expatriates leaving for holidays in India to take good-quality saris with them as gifts for people at home. In this way, a significant quantity of the saris imported into the Emirates from India actually find their way back to India.

CHAPTER 5

Silk-producing countries/areas

Brazil

Brazil is today the most important silk producer outside the traditional Asian silk-producing countries. It is the world's third largest silk producer after China and India. Raw silk production in the country in the silk year 1999 reached some 1,554 tons, 2% of world production. The declining trend of production continued in 2000: the raw silk output was 1,389 tons, 10.6% less than in 1999. The principal areas for sericulture are the States of São Paulo and Paraná, together accounting for about 96% of the country's silk output. Some sericulture is carried out in Santa Catarina and Mato Grosso do Sul, but the climate and soil in these areas are not as favourable.

The Brazilian silk year begins in September/October and ends in May; the following three months are too cold for mulberry harvesting. According to trade sources, harvesting can take place four times a year.

A comparison of the output of cocoons (estimated at 10,305 tons in 1999) with that of raw silk (about 1,554 tons in 1999) suggests a relatively high average yield per cocoon. This compares favourably with the figures reported for Japan and the Republic of Korea.

Production of silk in Brazil commenced in the 1920s. It was initially directed primarily to the local market. In the early 1970s, several Japanese trading houses looking for alternative supply sources established some silk production units in São Paulo and Paraná. Today sericulture and silk production in Brazil is practically controlled by Japanese interests. The three Brazilian raw silk and silk yarn producers are Bratac, Kanebo and Cocamar. The first two produce some 90% of the country's silk output. Japan is by far the most important customer for Brazilian silk and around 70% of all silk exports are directed to Japan.

In 1999 Brazil exported 1,287 tons of raw silk and 455 tons of silk yarn. Major recipients of Brazilian raw silk in 1999 were Japan (1,005 tons), India (163 tons), the Republic of Korea (143 tons), Switzerland (55 tons), France (101 tons) and Italy (20 tons). Japan imported some 364 tons of silk yarn from Brazil in 1999, which was its second biggest supplier after China (704 tons). Local consumption of silk in Brazil in 1999 was: raw silk 43 tons, thrown silk (silk yarn) 31 tons and silk waste 344 tons.

There is no doubt a flourishing, albeit small, domestic market for both ready-made and tailored silk garments. There are a few silk weavers in the country and most of them also have printing facilities. These weavers mainly supply local garment producers and the fairly large market for home sewing.

Most of the silk produced is exported as raw silk and silk yarn. Some silk fabrics are also exported – 95% are in the loom state, i.e. grey – and almost all are sent to Italy. Bratac, the country's leading silk producer, is one of the world's largest silk reelers. In 1999, it processed about 66% of Brazil's raw silk, and accounted for almost 68% of the national export trade in raw silk and silk yarn.

China

Sericulture

According to the China National Silk Import & Export Corporation (CNSIEC) the total acreage planted to mulberry in 1999 was about 597,600 hectares, 4.63% lower than the figure for the previous year (626,667 hectares). The production of mulberry cocoons (*Bombyx mori*) in 1999 amounted to 409,000 tons, down from 432,000 tons in 1998 (a fall of 8%). Raw silk production in 1999 was about 55,990 tons, more than 10% higher than the corresponding figure for 1998 (49,400 tons). In 2000 raw silk production in China reached 50,683 tons.

China's total silk exports climbed from US$ 1.1 billion in 1986 to US$ 2.9 billion in 1993. In 1996, however, the figure was lower at US$ 2.1 billion. According to Chinese Customs statistics, the value of Chinese exports of silk products was US$ 1.62 billion in 1999, down by 17.4% from 1998.

The main silk-producing provinces in China have traditionally been Sichuan, Zhejiang, Jiangsu and Guangdong. An estimated 20 million households are engaged in sericulture; an additional half a million people are employed by the country's 600 reeling and weaving mills. China's burgeoning industrial development is, however, affecting sericulture and silk production, particularly in Jiangsu and Zhejiang, which produce the country's best-quality silk. Some of the land devoted to sericulture has had to be reallocated to industrial use, motorways and housing development, and sericultural activities relocated to areas that may not have the best conditions for producing quality silk.

About 70% of the silk produced in China is bivoltine. It may be recalled that this silk is required in silk-producing developing countries to raise the quality of their fabrics to export standards.

China is also the world's largest producer of tussah, a wild silk. Production of tussah, which now reaches about 1,000 tons annually, takes place mainly in the northern province of Liaoning.

Silk production and exports

China today dominates world production of raw silk. As mentioned earlier, its output amounted to 55,990 tons of mulberry silk (almost 70% of the global production) and 1,000 tons of tussah in 1999. Chinese total silk exports in 1999 were 24,598 tons (an increase of 30.2% from 1998), out of which raw silk exports were 7,991 tons, 5.8% less than a year earlier.

In 1999 exports of silk fabrics were 100.5 million linear metres, out of which the exports of finished silk fabrics, i.e. printed or dyed, were 14.5 million metres. According to ITC Comtrade statistics Chinese silk fabric exports in 1999 reached some US$ 285 million, about 22% of the global silk fabric exports in that year.

Table 14 shows that the Chinese price for raw silk has been steadily going down and has remained at a very low level for the past few years.

Table 14 China: raw silk prices (20/22 denier), 1990–2000 (in US$/kg)

Year	US$/kg
1990	50
1993	31
1995	28
1998	27
2000	24

Source: ISA.

Exports of silk garments and other made-up goods were valued at US$ 852 million in 1999, 27.6% less than the 1998 figure. The European Union, one of China's leading markets for silk garments, imported 1,796 tons of these products in 1999, around 10% less than in 1998. According to Eurostat, the corresponding figure for imports of silk apparel and accessories from China in 1997 was 2,535 tons, out of which silk shirts accounted for 1,543 tons.

China's supplies to the United States rose rapidly from 850,000 dozen silk blouses and shirts in 1989 to 8.1 million dozen women's silk blouses (100% woven silk) in 1993. The growth rate between 1992 and 1993 alone was 129%. This trend was reversed in 1995/1996, with supplies dropping drastically in the aftermath of the sand-washed silk boom.

Table 15 is a significant proof of the continuous increase of silk processing in China. Until the mid 1980s the country was by and large the leading exporter of raw silk and silk yarn, which were then processed into finished products elsewhere in the world, e.g. in Europe. Since then China has begun to develop a silk-processing industry and, as the table indicates, today roughly half of China's silk exports falls into the category of finished products. This is naturally a very welcome development, particularly for the Chinese authorities, since export revenues will be growing this way. However, one must keep in mind that the quality requirements especially in Western markets and Japan are very high and therefore it is imperative that the exporting companies are aware of the market requirements.

Table 15 China: silk exports by product category, 1980–2000 (as percentage of total)

Year	Raw silk/silk yarn	Silk fabrics	Finished silk products
1980	49	34	17
1985	40	37	23
1990	29	31	40
1995	18	34	48
2000	33	17	49

Source: ISA.

This is becoming even more essential now, since the country has joined the WTO, which will eventually open doors into export markets for many more Chinese companies than before. Until now it has been primarily the trading houses that have been licensed to export silk and silk products. In the future, there will probably be more producers of silk products who will also be involved in direct exports.

According to the Hong Kong Customs Agency, Hong Kong (China) imported various silk products in 2000 as follows: finished silk products about 8,585 tons, silk fabrics 3,549 tons and spun silk yarn 2,004 tons. Total imports of silk products reached 15,646 tons. Re-exports amounted to 14,494 tons and 924 tons were exported. Local consumption was estimated at 228 tons. In 1999, the corresponding figures were slightly lower: total imports reached 15,520 tons, re-exports were 13,418 tons and exports 1,119 tons.

Over the last decade, the role of Hong Kong (China) has dramatically changed and today the Special Administrative Region (SAR) is more involved in financing the silk business in China, thus leaving the actual production more and more to the producers in China. No doubt there is still some fashion-related production of high quality silk garments, but the bulk production has been shifted away from Hong Kong (China).

Among China's successful new products are knitted goods, particularly sweaters made of silk, often blended with other textile fibres such as cotton, linen and ramie.

One factor that will have to be taken seriously into consideration in assessing the future availability of Chinese silk in international markets is the gradually growing domestic demand for silk products. While it is true that the monthly incomes of consumers even in the more affluent coastal areas remain modest, the shift to large-scale consumerism in the silk sector is bound to occur in the not-too-distant future. One reason for this increase in demand is the reduction in raw silk prices in China from US$ 50/kg in 1990 to US$ 24/kg in 2000 (see table 14).

India

Sericulture

India has long traditions of sericulture, going back to the second century BC. Sericulture flourished from the eighteenth to early twentieth century during British rule. Silk has had a central role in Indian culture and long traditions of wearing silk still prevail in the country. The silk industry in India is essentially a cottage industry and the sericulture is mainly left to small and marginal farmers. Sericulture and silk production are considered as one of the potential tools for the improvement of economic conditions in rural areas. It is estimated that this sector offers employment opportunities to some 6.3 million people. India has the distinction of being the only country in the world to produce all the commercially known varieties of silk – mulberry, *tasar* (both tropical and temperate), *eri* and *muga*. In 1999 it ranked second to China as a mulberry silk producer and accounts for more than 17% of world production of raw silk, or 13,944 tons out of the total production of 76,300 tons. It is also the second largest producer of *tasar* silk, again after China. It monopolizes production of the golden-yellow *muga* silk.

As mentioned earlier, sericulture is a cottage industry in some 59,000 villages in India. Mulberry sericulture takes place mainly in Karnataka, Andhra Pradesh, Tamil Nadu, Jammu and Kashmir and West Bengal, which account for about 99% of all the mulberry raw silk produced in the country. In addition to being suitable for marginal land, sericulture has the advantage of having an end product with good export potential. It is also one of the most labour-intensive sectors of the Indian economy, providing full-time and part-time employment to approximately 6 million individuals. The industry has been identified as one of the thrust sectors of the economy in view of its potential for employment generation and the vital role it plays in transferring wealth from the richer to the poorer sections of the population. A summary of the distribution of the proceeds from sales of soft silk fabrics weighing 40, 50 and 60 grams per metre among workers in the silk industry is given in table 16.

Overall responsibility for the development of the sericulture industry has been entrusted to the Central Silk Board (CSB), a statutory body constituted in 1949 by Act of Parliament. The Board is under the administrative control of the Ministry of Textiles. CSB coordinates the development of sericulture in various States and is directly responsible for research, training, seed production, price stabilization for cocoons and raw silk, standardization and quality control for silk products, and for advising the Central Government on all matters relating to the silk industry, including import/export policy. The Board has a network of 233 research, extension and seed units all over the country. It also has eight certification centres for the pre-shipment inspection of silk products intended for export. Among the research units is the Central Sericulture Research Institute, which was established in Mysore in 1961, initially as a research and development centre for the southern States. It has since gained national status. More recently it has been training personnel from other developing countries in cooperation with the International Centre for Training and Research in Tropical Sericulture (ICTRETS). The Centre, also located in Mysore, was established in 1980 under the auspices of the Indo-Swiss Technical and Scientific Cooperation.

Production of raw silk in India was some 1,214 tons in 1950 and it has been increasing steadily from between 1,250 and 1,650 tons annually of multivoltine silk in the mid 1970s to today's 13,000–14,000 tons. The total raw silk production in 2000 was about 15,214 tons, showing an increase of almost 10% from 1999. India is today the second largest producer of mulberry silk in the world.

Table 16 India: percentage distribution of proceeds from sales of soft silk fabrics, by category of worker (as percentage of total)

Category of work	Weight of fabric (Grams per metre)		
	40	50	60
Total of which:	**100.0**	**100.0**	**100.0**
Cocoon producer	51.5	54.6	56.8
Reeler	6.2	6.6	6.8
Twister	8.2	8.7	9.1
Weaver	14.5	12.3	10.7
Trader	19.5	17.8	16.6

Source: ITC, *Silk Review 1997.*

Silk processing

According to the Central Silk Board in November 2000, India's silk-reeling capacity in the silk year 1999/2000 consisted of 32,697 charkas (hand-driven reeling machines), and 25,645 cottage and filature basins. It has about 200,000 twisting spindles, mostly in small factories. Silk fabrics in India are woven on both hand-looms and power looms. There are some 227,000 hand-looms and 29,300 power looms in the country.

The output of fabrics is made up mainly of saris, dress materials and furnishing fabrics. About 90% of the silk produced for the domestic market is for saris, which are woven mainly in the States of Tamil Nadu, Karnataka, Andhra Pradesh, Uttar Pradesh, West Bengal, Orissa, and Jammu and Kashmir. Among the centres producing other fabrics are Bangalore (Karnataka), Champa (Madhya Pradesh), Bhagalpur (Bihar) and Navpatna (Orissa).

The Government has established centralized services for the weaving industry in various parts of the country. The centres provide assistance on such matters as weaving techniques, design and product development.

Among the large variety of silk goods produced for the domestic and external markets are mixed/blended silk fabrics, dress fabrics, saris, scarves and stoles, made-up articles (cushion covers, bedspreads), silk carpets and silk garments.

Domestic consumption

India has a large domestic market for silk goods and only some 15% of production is exported. About 85% of the silk goods sold on the domestic market consist of traditional items such as saris, sari blouses and dhotis.

The current raw silk output falls short of demand. In order to supplement domestic production, India imported 5,018 tons of raw silk in 1999/2000, valued at US$ 95 million, mostly from China (4,581 tons), Hong Kong (China) (203 tons) and Brazil (107 tons). In the silk year 2000/01, India imported some 4,700 tons for US$ 88.3 million. Efforts are also being made to increase domestic production. Both bilateral agencies (the Swiss Agency for Development and Cooperation) and international financial institutions (World Bank) have assisted India in these efforts. They have also provided assistance in the upgrading of infrastructure and technology to enable the sector to meet the increasing domestic and export demand for silk products. One such effort was the National Sericulture Project, launched with the assistance of the World Bank and Switzerland. Its aim was to raise production of raw mulberry silk from around 10,000 tons to 20,000 tons. The implementing agencies under the project were the five traditional silk-growing States of Karnataka, Andhra Pradesh, Tamil Nadu, West Bengal, Jammu and Kashmir, and the Central Silk Board.

Any additional output will go largely towards meeting the steadily growing domestic demand for silk products. India has an estimated 220 million customary users of silk. Rising standards of living will mean increased demand for silk goods.

As mentioned earlier, India mainly produces multivoltine silk. It requires yarn from bivoltine silk (which does not break) for the power-loom industry to expand. In order to satisfy the growing demand for silk for lighter-weight clothing (such as blouses, shirts, dresses, saris), the Government has allowed since the late 1980s imports of bivoltine raw silk or silk yarn. This is used as warp in hand-loomed fabrics and as warp and weft in power-loomed goods.

The total demand for silk has reached about 21,000 tons, of which about two-thirds are supplied from domestic sources. Recently India has liberalized imports of raw silk and silk yarn, since the local production was not large enough to cater for the needs of the Indian silk-processing industry. The steadily rising domestic demand for silk products may well mean no significant expansion in India's export trade. The shortfall in domestic supplies may have to be met by imports of silk and other competing fabrics and made-up products, when this trade is liberalized under WTO rules.

Exports

About 15% of India's output of all types of silk goods is exported. The latest export figures show that foreign exchange earnings through silk exports are progressing satisfactorily. According to the Central Silk Board, Bangalore, in 1999/2000 the total value of silk exports was 175,555 lakhs of Indian rupees, around US$ 405 million (1 lakh = 100,000). The estimated figures for 2000/01 are 242,132 lakhs of rupees or US$ 429.6 million. It is interesting to note that silk garment exports seem to be increasing fast. In1999/2000 the value of silk garment exports was US$ 86.2 million and for the following year the estimated value is US$ 186.6 million. In the silk year 1999/2000 some 80% of tasar and mulberry silk fabrics exported from India were woven by power looms and the rest by hand-looms.

India's exports consist exclusively of saris, dress fabrics, ready-made garments and made-up articles for interior decoration (e.g. bedspreads, cushion covers, curtains). In 1999/2000 'silk garments' was the second biggest product category (in quantity) of mulberry silk goods exports (10%), after dress fabrics (almost 70%). Recent reports also indicate that India is gradually beginning to export knitted silk items as well, this product group being one of the new potentially interesting ones in international silk business.

India's export trade is highly concentrated, with the 10 leading buyers taking more than 80% of its trade in mulberry silk goods. The value of exports in this category was 114,287.57 lakhs of Indian rupees. The shares of some of the largest markets in 1999/2000 for this category were: United States 30.5%, Germany 14.9%, United Kingdom 12.7%, Italy 7.98%, France 6.28%, Spain 3.68% and Japan 2.01%.

The types of product of interest to individual markets vary. The most important product category in the United Arab Emirates, Mauritius and Singapore is the sari, and this is due to the presence in these countries of a sizeable ethnic community from the Indian subcontinent.

India's share in the global silk export trade continues to be fairly insignificant in relation to the country's position as the world's second largest producer and the biggest importer of raw silk. This does not, however, mean that Indian silk products could not have a higher market share in some specific product groups and markets. There is no doubt a steady international clientele for traditional Indian fabrics such as dupion. This demand will continue but suppliers should keep in mind that it is absolutely vital to deliver the qualities contracted.

Most probably it is in the interest of many Indian silk weavers to continue to produce silk fabrics by hand-loom, because this will help to prevent direct competition with finished silk products from China in international markets. However, some of the more modern silk-weaving mills in India have successfully marketed fabrics in qualities (satins and taffetas) that have been supplied primarily by China. This has encouraged some European enterprises to enter into joint ventures with Indian partners for the production of these fabrics.

Indian exporters will have to follow very carefully, through the Central Silk Board and the Indian Silk Export Promotion Council (ISEPC), any new or forthcoming legislation on products and production methods particularly in the European Union. ISEPC was established by the Government in June 1983 as the registering authority for exporters of silk products. It replaced diversified export promotion councils, such as the Apparels Export Promotion Council and the Rayon and Silk Export Promotion Council. More than 1,400 exporters are registered with ISEPC.

The Council publishes a weekly bulletin (*Silknet*) which provides useful information on the markets for, and the marketing of, silk products, as well as statistical information on production and trade.

Republic of Korea

Like its neighbours, the Republic of Korea has a long tradition as a producer of silk. However, as it develops into a considerable industrial power, it is becoming increasingly difficult for it to retain land for mulberry cultivation and to find the manpower for the labour-intensive processes of cocoon and raw-silk production. As a result, production of cocoons, once amounting to 41,000 tons, has fallen to a minimal level; in 1996 this was about 520 tons. The production of raw silk in 1996 was 146 tons; the corresponding figure in 1999 was 50 tons.

The shortfall in the domestic supply of raw silk and silk yarn has prompted silk processors in the Republic to look for new potential suppliers of these products. Possibilities for sericulture have been explored in several Latin American countries. Similarly, joint ventures have started in Viet Nam to assist in the rehabilitation of sericulture and silk production in that country. Some silk-reeling mills have been relocated from the Republic of Korea to Viet Nam.

The Republic's silk-processing industry has been developing apace. In general, this development has followed the Japanese pattern. One reason for this has been cooperation between its weavers and Japanese traders in the production of fabrics, which had to meet Japan's stringent quality requirements for kimonos. The technical skills thus acquired over the years have enabled the country to produce other types of fabrics (including crêpe de Chine) for export.

Over the past few years the country's silk-processing industry has reached quality levels enabling it to take a strong position in many markets.

According to Comtrade statistics the Republic of Korea had a share of about 18% of global silk fabric exports in 1999. The value of these exports was estimated at US$ 138.2 million. Comtrade statistics also indicate that the Republic of Korea had a share of 11% of silk fabric market in the United States in 1999 valued at US$ 27.3 million (286 tons).

Production of made-up silk goods such as neckties and scarves has also reached the quality standards demanded by Japanese buyers and cooperation between the two countries in this area is expected to continue. This quality improvement and the country's proximity to the Japanese market will continue to induce Japanese buyers to import a variety of silk goods from the Republic of Korea. According to the Ministry of Finance of Japan, however, imports into Japan of Korean silk fabrics have been declining lately. In 1996 silk fabric imports from the Republic of Korea were some 6.6 million m^2 but the corresponding figure for the year 1999 was only 1.57 million m^2. A similar trend can be found in silk yarn exports to Japan: in 1993 Japan imported some 763 tons of Korean silk yarn; in 1999 imports reached only 187 tons. According to Japanese sources this decline is mainly due to the decreasing demand for traditional Japanese style silk goods, mainly kimonos.

The industry as it stands today consists of fairly large production units, which means that minimum orders per style have to be bigger than in some competing countries. A major silk exporter indicated that the minimum order for one fabric design in four colours is 1,000 yards (250 yards per colour). For garments, the minimum order per style is 500 pieces. This feature makes silk products from the Republic of Korea more easily marketed in the United States and in Japan – the world's largest silk-consumers. By contrast, European buyers may find the large minimum quantities a serious obstacle to trade.

Imports. To meet the requirements of its vibrant silk-processing industry, the Republic imports mainly silk yarn and, particularly, loomstate silk fabrics. The main suppliers of woven silk fabrics are China, Hong Kong (China) and Italy.

The country's silk processors are always on the lookout for additional supply sources of raw materials and often collaborate with local entrepreneurs in various parts of the world.

Overall, according to the Korean Sericulture Association, the Republic of Korea is no longer a silk producer, but the country imported some 1,700 tons of raw silk and 2,500 tons of silk fabrics in the year 2000. Exports the same year reached 1,800 tons of silk fabrics and 2,100 tons of finished silk goods. The country's long tradition in processing silk into finished products is now being done with the help of imports of raw materials.

Thailand

Sericulture. Although Thailand has been producing silk for more than a thousand years, production in volume only began early in the twentieth century. It is today among the world's leading producers of raw silk. Its output consists mainly of multivoltine silk for weft yarns. The annual production of multivoltine silk was more than 1,000 tons in the mid 1990s.

In 1999 mulberry silk production was 1,000 tons; in 2000 production reached 955 tons of raw silk. A limited quantity of bivoltine silk for good quality warp yarn is also produced domestically (some 350 tons in 1998), but domestic demand must be complimented by imports, mainly from China.

Government sources indicate that domestic supplies of raw material are currently sufficient for only 70% of demand; the country spends more than baht 500 million annually on imports of silk yarn, mainly from China, Viet Nam and India.

In 1994 the European Union allocated baht 400 million for a five-year project to support mulberry growing and sericulture in Thailand.

Processing and trade. About 350,000 households in the northern and north-eastern parts of the country rely on sericulture for additional income. Silk reeling is carried out by hand by village women. The yarn is uneven and has knots that, together with a certain wavy appearance, give Thai silk fabrics a unique texture, which many overseas buyers find attractive.

The fabrics are generally yarn dyed. In addition, some fabric printing takes place and Thailand has been exporting quality printed silk fabrics or selling them to tourists. Some fabrics, like *mud mee* and the intricate *ikat* silks, are representative of the country's culture and illustrate the special skills of the Thai weaver.

While the country has a number of silk factories, the weaving of fabrics remains basically a cottage industry, with thousands of households deriving all or part of their income from it. The north-east remains the main centre of production, but silk fabrics are also produced in other parts of the country. Most fabrics are plain woven on hand-looms. Some quality fabrics for kimonos are produced on power looms for export to the Japanese market. As in India, Thai silk weavers are increasingly producing silk fabrics using modern power looms. One of the few producers of jacquard silk fabrics is Thai Silk Co. Ltd, which makes these fabrics mainly for interior decoration.

A significant proportion of the country's exports of silk goods consists of sales to foreign tourists visiting Thailand. Gift items continue to sell well, and neckties, scarves and cushion covers make up an estimated 50% of the country's silk exports. One factor that had been in Thailand's favour has been the skilful printing of hand-loom silk fabrics.

Domestic demand for silk products is fairly high. The items sold locally include shirts, dressing gowns, skirts, sarongs, scarves, neckties, cushion covers, pillow cases, bedspreads, tablecloths, table-mats and curtains. Thailand imports silk fabrics as well as silk garments for retail in local stores.

Viet Nam

Vietnamese sericulture began more than 3,000 years ago, probably under the influence of China, and has been practised ever since by most village families, largely for their own use and for the domestic market. Exports of silk products were started with the arrival of the French about 150 years ago and continued until the Second World War, when about 85% of the 10,000 hectares of land devoted to sericulture was diverted to food crops. Viet Nam subsequently managed to regain these hectares for mulberry cultivation. However, the results of the first five years were not encouraging, largely owing to the lack of tools and technology. In 1985, the Government launched the Silk Integrated Agro Project for the promotion of sericulture. The Viet Nam Union of Sericulture Enterprises (VISERI) was established in Bao Loc as the agency responsible for sericulture management, development and trade. VISERI is part of the Ministry of Agriculture and Food Industry.

Bao Loc is not the only silk production centre in Viet Nam, but the climatic conditions in the Lam Dong highlands certainly make it one of the country's most suitable areas for sericulture. Many areas which are now used for growing coffee or tea could easily be used for sericulture. The subtropical climate (22°C–29°C) contributes to the availability of fresh mulberry leaves all year round, making cropping possible 12 times a year. Sericulture is labour intensive and one-hectare farms employ about 10 people. Elsewhere in the country, fresh leaves are not to be had for about three months in the year because of heavy rains or extreme heat, and cropping can be carried out only 7 – 8 times yearly.

The national output of raw silk rose from 420 tons in 1990 to 1,000 tons in 1992 and 1,500 tons in 1996. Production under VISERI likewise grew from 350 tons in 1991 to 1,000 tons in 1994. It is estimated that 80% of the country's raw silk will come from Lam Dong province in the future. Lately the national production figures for raw silk have steadily declined: in 1995 the output was some 2,100 tons, in 1996 some 1,500 tons, in 1997 some 860 tons and in 1999 only 780 tons of raw silk. It is hoped that the production figures for raw silk will soon start growing again. Latest data from the Ministry of Agriculture, Forestry and Fisheries (MAFF), Tokyo, Japan indicate that Viet Nam has been exporting increasing quantities of silk yarn to the Japanese market. In 2000 the amount was 375 tons, whereas a year earlier the corresponding figure was just 195 tons. In 1995 Viet Nam exported only 2 tons of silk yarn to Japan. This growth is encouraging, since it shows that the silk processing in the country is improving.

Several countries and institutions are actively involved with the silk industry in Viet Nam. They include the Republic of Korea (which has reeling mills in Viet Nam), Italy and the World Bank, which has carried out a general survey of sericulture in Viet Nam.

VISERI has been engaged in efforts to improve the quality of its raw silk and to upgrade its silk-processing facilities. It has attracted the attention of various foreign companies who have established joint ventures with it.

Viet Nam is expected to develop into an important international supplier of raw silk and silk yarn. The development of its weaving industry will have a considerable effect on the export performance of its garment industry.

Domestic demand, currently still fairly dormant, should grow as standards of living rise.

Other silk-producing countries/areas

This section provides some information on a number of countries and areas that are currently producing small quantities of raw silk.

Africa

In December 1999 the future potential for sericulture and silk production was discussed at the 2nd International Workshop on the Conservation and Utilisation of Commercial Insects in Nairobi, Kenya. The workshop was organized by and held at the International Centre of Insect Physiology and Ecology (ICIPE). Participants from various parts of the world discussed the so far largely untapped potential for sericulture in African hemisphere. Some of the findings of the workshop are listed below:

- Climatically many African countries are well-suited for cultivation and rearing of silkworms.
- Agriculture is still the main occupation of people and the socio-economic conditions seem to be favourable for sericulture.
- The mulberry tree is drought resistant and an ideal crop in the arid and semi-arid lands of Kenya.
- ICIPE has established training groups in Kenya both for sericulture and silk production.
- The Uganda experience: since the mid 1990s the European Union has sponsored activity for the production of mulberry silk cocoons. As a result of the project, a few tons of cocoons were produced, but it was economically feasible to export the cocoons. At the same time there was no existing silk-processing facility in the country; i.e. it is indispensable to have at least some reeling capacity for raw silk in the country.

- It was generally acknowledged that there would be reasonable local demand in many African countries for silk fabrics.
- In the past there have been efforts to launch sericultural activities in several African countries, such as Botswana, Kenya, Nigeria, Zambia and Zimbabwe, but for a variety of reasons the success has been rather limited.

Bangladesh

Bangladesh has a long tradition in sericulture and in the production of silk products. For a variety of reasons the silk output, however, suffered a steep decline in the twentieth century. Consequently, domestic production of both raw silk and fabrics falls far below domestic demand. In order to revive the sector, the Government decided to embark on the Bangladesh Silk Development Project (BSDP) with a support of a credit from the World Bank/IDA amounting to some US$ 11.3 million. The implementation of the project is entrusted to the Bangladesh Silk Foundation (BSF), which was established following the approval of the credit.

The country's output of raw silk is estimated at some 30 tons a year with a target of 180 tons in the year 2002, the year the project will be ending. The raw silk currently produced in the country is suitable only for weft and therefore Bangladesh must import high quality silk for warp yarn, up to about 300 tons per year from China, India, Uzbekistan and Viet Nam. According to the Bangladesh Silk Foundation the availability of silk fabrics in 1998/99 was some 3.3 million metres, up from 1.9 million metres in 1996/97. The yearly output of silk fabrics is insufficient and the rest of the demand has to be met by imports. The BSF estimated that about 30% of the local demand for saris could be met by local production by the end of the BSDP.

Colombia

Sericultural activities started in Colombia more than twenty years ago and they were first targeted to the Japanese for exports of dried cocoons from Colombia. In 1994 some 400 hectares were under mulberry cultivation and cocoon production reached 235 tons. Raw silk production in that year amounted to 36.7 tons. Cocoon production dropped down to 35 tons in 1998, but the following year production increased by 78% up to some 62 tons of mulberry cocoons.

Egypt

In Egypt silk is steadily in demand for the production of hand-knotted silk carpets. In 2001 the production of raw silk reached some 15 tons.

Japan

According to the Japan Silk Association, Japan had a consumption of some 14,000 tons of silk products in 1999 and its raw silk production in 2000 was less than 600 tons. The former silk producer has become a large importer of silk products, although it still has silk projects linked to research and promotion.

Table 17 indicates how the Japanese market price for raw silk has plummeted over a ten-year period. Raw silk demand in Japan has been significantly reduced by the simple fact that local silk processing has been increasingly replaced by imports of finished silk goods, particularly from China and some other countries in the region.

Table 17 Japan: raw silk prices (27/29 denier), 1990–2000 (in US$/kg)

1990	110
1993	102
1995	28
1998	27
2000	24

Source: ISA.

Nepal

Nepal is an aspiring silk producer. It has no traditions in the silk industry but, as experts from Japan and the Republic of Korea pointed out in the 1970s, it has favourable agro-climatic and socio-economic conditions for sericulture.

In 1975, the Industrial Entomology Project (IEP) was set up in Kopasi, near Kathmandu, with the assistance of sericulture experts from the Republic of Korea. In 1994, the Silk Association of Nepal (SAN) was established to promote the development of sericulture and the silk industry.

United Kingdom

The Silk Association of Great Britain has indicated that local silk processing is concentrating on the production of silk fabrics for neckties and for interior decoration. The Association is also involved with silk promotion activities directed to schools and universities, especially in the area of design.

Uzbekistan

The collapse of the Soviet Union deprived Uzbekistan of some of its traditional markets for silk and silk products. The sector is gradually recovering and the latest news from Uzbekistan indicate that silk production is being revitalized. In order to improve the sericulture and silk production in the country the Uzbek Ipagi Association was created in March 1998 by the decree of the President of the country. This association has united all silk-processing enterprises under the Ministry of Agriculture and Uzbeklegprom Association. The Uzbek Ipagi Association is carrying out work to increase the production of the silk industry, to improve the quality and to enlarge the export potential of the enterprises.

Cocoon production, which was about 33,000 tons in 1992, has dropped down to about 20,000 tons. In 1999 the cocoon output was 18,873 tons and in 2000 the corresponding figure was 20,500 tons.

Raw silk production is improving and in 2000 was some 1,100 tons; the output in 1998 was only 556 tons. The production of silk yarn is also increasing: in

1998 22.3 tons were produced and in 2000 some 140 tons. Latest information from Uzbekistan also indicates that further processing of silk yarn into silk fabrics and finished products is on the increase.

Uzbekistan has a long tradition in sericulture and the silk production and exports are showing an encouraging upward trend. Trade links have been established with a number of Asian countries, including China, as well as the United States and Europe. The local Silk Association aims to reach 3A quality level in the foreseeable future.

If the raw silk output continues to rise steadily, Uzbekistan may well develop into an interesting new supplier of silk in export markets, since its raw silk output could soon match that of Brazil.

Conclusions

China is the de facto leader for silk production transformation and trade. It must be kept in mind that China's accession to the WTO will gradually liberalize the local market as well. The Chinese are interested in upgrading of silk products and are also willing to develop silk research and modernize the image of silk. India is gradually improving its quality of mulberry sericulture and research is progressing. Brazil will continue to aim at top quality production and exports.

Former producers of silk, such as Japan and the Republic of Korea, are concentrating on research and new technologies in cooperation with the International Sericulture Commission.

European and American silk processors and traders are defending their positions regarding legal matters, such as copyrights and intellectual property laws and they urge a wider cooperation between countries for fairer trade.